TRAIL TOOLS

* **Trail Maps**
* **Trail Profiles**
* **Destination Charts**
* **Mileage Charts**

For Hikers and Backpackers

Yosemite Valley

By Dennis V. O'Neill

Published By

O'Neill Software

P.O. Box 26111
San Francisco, CA 94126

Phone: 415/398-2255
Email: oneillsw@hooked.net

Trail Tools: Yosemite Valley
Trail Maps, Trail Profiles, Mileage Charts, and Destination Charts
for Hikers and Backpackers

By Dennis V. O'Neill

Published By
O'Neill Software
P.O. Box 26111
San Francisco, CA 94126

Phone: 415/398-2255
Email: oneillsw@hooked.net

First Edition

Library of Congress Cataloging-in-Publication Data

O'Neill, Dennis V.
Trail Tools: Yosemite Valley / by Dennis V. O'Neill
144 p. 28 cm.
Includes maps, illustrations, index.
ISBN 0-931285-05-4 : $12.95
1. Hiking — California — Yosemite National Park — Guidebooks
2. Backpacking — California — Yosemite National Park — Guidebooks
3. Trails — California — Yosemite National Park — Guidebooks
4. Yosemite National Park (Calif.) — Guidebooks
5. Wilderness Areas — California — Guidebooks
917.9447

Library of Congress Catalog Card Number: 96-92038

TABLE OF CONTENTS

See Key Map on page 9 for trailhead locations

See Key Map on page 9 for trailhead locations

CHAPTER 1: INTRODUCTION

1.1 USES

This book is designed for hikers, backpackers, and others who use the Yosemite Valley trails. Like a map, it can be used every time you hike. Here are some ways *Trail Tools* can help you:

- *Plan Trips*: All the tools you need to plan a trip are here, in one place. Maps show where the trails go, profiles and charts show what it will be like to get there.

- *Compare Alternative Routes Visually*: Compare actual distance and difficulty just by flipping pages.

- *Make Reliable Decisions*: Base your decisions on accurate, factual data — not guesses.

- *Evaluate Trail Difficulty*: Know what to expect before you hike. Each mile is rated for difficulty.

- *Estimate Hiking Time*: Easily determine how fast you can get to any destination.

- *Chart On-Trail Progress*: Tell where you are; see how far you must go. If you look at a trail profile after you reach your first trail junction, you will instantly understand what the rest of the trail will be like in comparison.

- *Keep Records of Trips*: Once you've hiked a profiled trail, you can quickly judge how much easier or harder any other trail will be.

1.2 FEATURES

This book provides accurate trail information in a variety of useful formats. Here are some features you should note:

- *Measured Trail Distances*: Distances shown are actual, measured, on-trail distances, not estimates. Trails with switchbacks are shown at full length.

- *Real Elevations*: Every elevation change of 40 feet or more is included. Elevations can be cross-referenced to the real world, to USGS maps, and to other topographic maps.

- *Precision and Accuracy*: All tools are computer-generated for precision and accuracy.

- *Visual Cross-Referencing*: Maps, profiles, and charts are placed side-by-side across two facing pages. Cross-reference point to point with ease.

- *Thorough Indexes*: Look up any on-trail location and quickly find every trail that goes to it.

- *Complete Routes*: Trails are shown from trailhead to destination, not in small segments.

- *Logical Order*: Alternative routes from each trailhead are shown one after the other, in sequence.

1.3 BOOK COVERAGE

This book covers all maintained trails leading to and from Yosemite Valley. It covers the area from the Valley north to Tioga Road and the Valley south to Glacier Point Road. Trails along the Valley floor, which are essentially level, are not profiled.

1.4 CUSTOM TRAIL TOOLS

You can order custom-designed *Trail Tools* based on any route you choose. Copy any of the maps in this book, mark your route on the map, and fax or mail it for a price quote. Use the form on page 143 to make ordering easier.

1.5 COMMENTS WELCOME

Please send comments, questions, corrections, and suggestions to Dennis O'Neill at:

Mail:	O'Neill Software, P.O. Box 26111, San Francisco, CA 94126.
Email:	oneillsw@hooked.net.
Phone:	415/398-2255 (between 8 AM and 5 PM Pacific time).

1.6 CAUTION

- The material in this book is intended for recreational use, to supplement information provided by maps and guidebooks. It is not a replacement for other sources of information.

- This book focuses on trail characteristics that can be measured and compared. There are many other trail characteristics, not as easily measured, that must also be considered when choosing between trails.

- Some of the trails profiled in this book may be hard to locate and difficult to follow. Trails may be closed or re-routed. Trail conditions can vary considerably, depending on the seasons, weather, and other factors. They can sometimes be dangerous. There may be mistakes in this book. For these and other reasons, you must review other sources of information and discuss your travel plans with people who know the area before heading into the backcountry.

- Permits are required for overnight backpack trips in Yosemite. You must know and comply with the regulations established by the National Park Service when using the park.

- Some trails are included in this book for completeness, not because they are recommended hiking trails. Other existing trails have been omitted because they are not maintained, not shown on USGS maps, are too short, or because they are similar to, or adjacent to, a profiled trail.

1.7 PROTECT OUR WILDERNESS

Wilderness areas were set aside by congress as places where nature exists in its pristine condition, unchanged by humans. Thousands of people before you have left these areas unspoiled, so you can enjoy them now. Please continue the tradition. There are many ways to protect our wilderness. Some ways are obvious; some are not. The staff at the Visitor Center listed below can make recommendations. Other organizations you can contact are listed in the Appendix on page 137.

1.8 YOSEMITE NATIONAL PARK INFORMATION

For information about Yosemite National Park, contact:

Yosemite Valley Visitor Center
Yosemite Village
P.O. Box 577
Yosemite, CA 95389
209/372-0200 (phone messaging system)

CHAPTER 2: TRAIL TOOLS

2.1 OVERVIEW

Trail Tools shows each trail from four different perspectives: As a cross-sectional Trail Profile, as a route highlighted on a Trail Map, as a listing in a Destination Chart, and as a listing in a Mileage Chart. Although based on exactly the same points, each view appears radically different and has a different purpose.

2.2 TRAIL PROFILES

A Trail Profile tracks a trail along its route, showing distance and elevation at each point. All profiles are the same scale so they can be visually compared. Features along the trail are precisely located so you can see how they relate to each other, vertically and horizontally.

2.3 TRAIL MAPS

A Trail Map shows relationships between the trail being profiled and other features on the terrain. The profiled trail is shown as a series of black dots spaced one-tenth of a mile apart. Distance from the trailhead is shown in miles as a large dot with a mileage number alongside.

2.4 DESTINATION CHARTS

A Destination Chart lists significant features along a trail and tells how far each is from the trailhead. Distances given are on-trail distances, horizontal and vertical -- distances you actually hike, not just distances between points. You can use Destination Charts to accurately estimate hiking time.

2.5 MILEAGE CHARTS

A Mileage Chart shows elevation gain and loss on a per mile-basis. In effect, a Mileage Chart provides a rating system for each mile along the trail. You can compare individual miles or entire trail segments.

2.6 SYMBOLS

Refer to the map legend and abbreviations on page 8 for an explanation of the symbols used.

2.7 KEY MAP

The Key Map on page 9 should be the starting point for most of your trips. It shows where all trails originate. Each trailhead is designated by a number within a circle.

2.8 CROSS REFERENCES

Trail junctions and other features are each assigned a unique Location Number for easy cross referencing. Use Index A to find an on-trail feature by Location Number, or Index B to find a feature by its name. Both indexes give you a list of all trails that go to or by the point you are looking for.

2.9 USING TRAIL TOOLS

Chapter 3, beginning on page 124, shows how to effectively use the maps, profiles, and charts in this book.

Map Legend

....	Trail
2 ↙	Mileage Marker, for cross-reference between Map, Profile, and Mileage Chart
●●●●●●●●●●● ● ● ● ●	Trail being profiled. Dots are 1/10 mile apart.
248 ↙	Location Number, for cross-reference between Map, Profile, and Destination Chart
....	Stream
——————————	Highway or primary road
———————————	Secondary Road
- - - - - - - - - - - - -	Tunnel
⑨	Trailhead
◈ 9	Trailhead of trail being profiled
△	Peak
1A	Trail Number. Number indicates trailhead. Letter indicates destination.
P	Parking

Abbreviations

CG	Campground
HSC	High Sierra Camp
L	Lake
LYV	Little Yosemite Valley
Mdw	Meadow
Rd	Road
Rt	Route
Tr	Trail

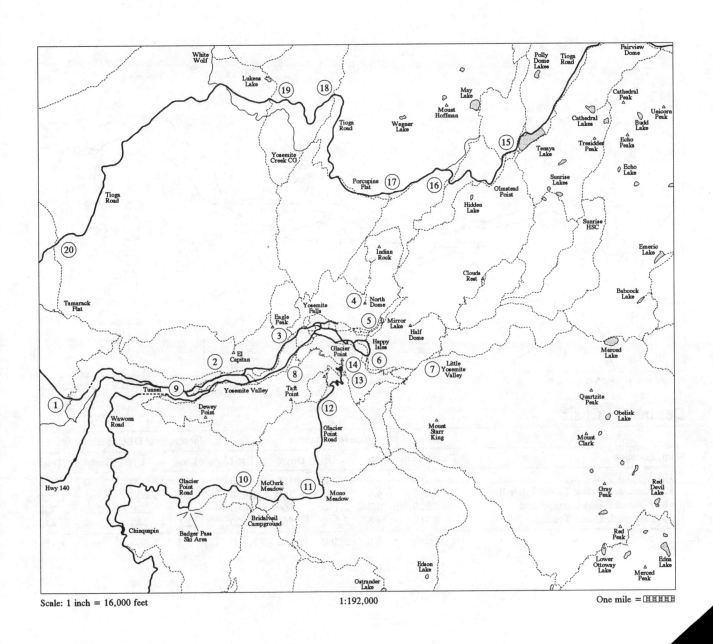

Scale: 1 inch = 16,000 feet   1:192,000   One mile = ⊞⊞⊞⊞⊞

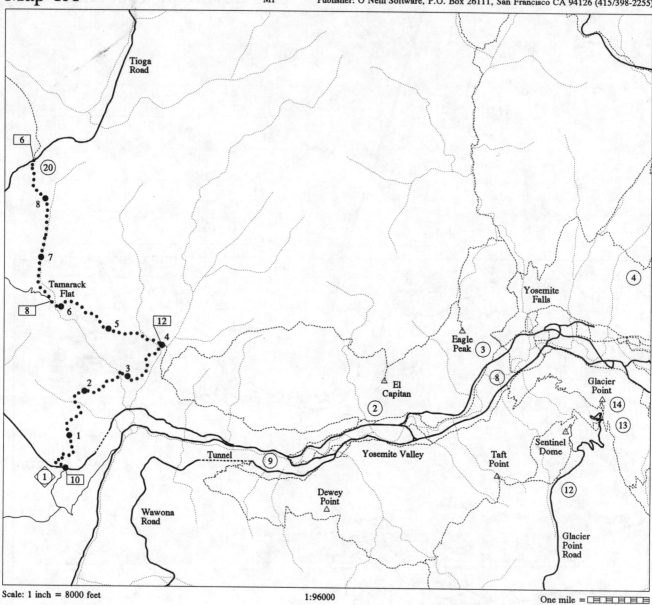

Scale: 1 inch = 8000 feet　　　　　　1:96000　　　　　　One mile =

Destination Chart

Num	Location	Elevation	Cumulative Distances				Incremental Distances			
			Miles	Up	Down	Total	Miles	Up	Down	Total
10	Big Oak Flat Road	4,760	0.0	0	0	0	0.0	0	0	0
12	Tamarack Creek Tr/Rockslide Rt	6,000	4.0	1,600	360	1,960	4.0	1,600	360	1,960
8	Tamarack Flat Campground	6,320	6.2	2,120	560	2,680	2.2	520	200	720
6	Tamarack Creek Trailhead	6,760	8.8	2,560	560	3,120	2.6	440	0	440
	Totals		8.8	2,560	560	3,120	8.8	2,560	560	3,120

Publisher: O'Neill Software, P.O. Box 26111, San Francisco CA 94126 (415/398-2255)

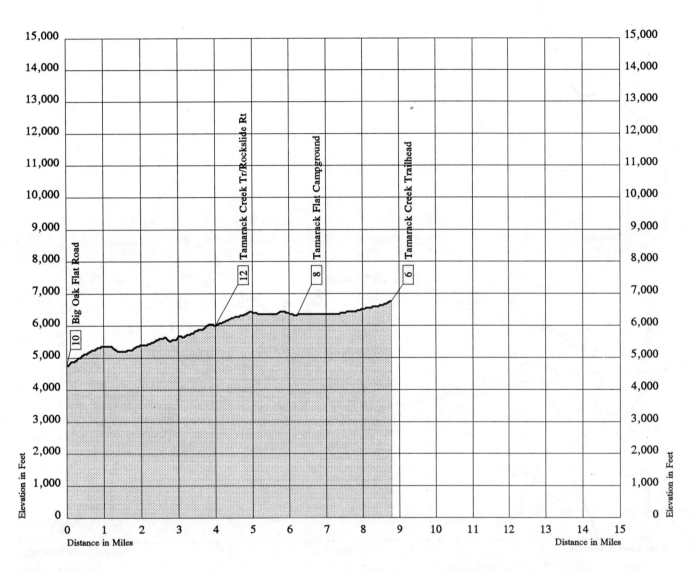

Mileage Chart

Mile	Elevation	Cumulative Distances			Incremental Distances		
		Up	Down	Rating	Up	Down	Rating
0	4,760	0	0	0	0	0	0
1	5,360	600	0	600	600	0	600
2	5,400	800	160	960	200	160	360
3	5,640	1,160	280	1,440	360	120	480
4	6,000	1,600	360	1,960	440	80	520
5	6,400	2,040	400	2,440	440	40	480
6	6,360	2,120	520	2,640	80	120	200
7	6,360	2,160	560	2,720	40	40	80
8	6,520	2,320	560	2,880	160	0	160
8.8	6,760	2,560	560	3,120	240	0	240
8.8	Totals	2,560	560	3,120	2,560	560	3,120

Notes

Route:
  10 to 6:   Tamarack Creek Trail

Trail from 12 to 6 not measured
See 20A for opposite direction

Map Location

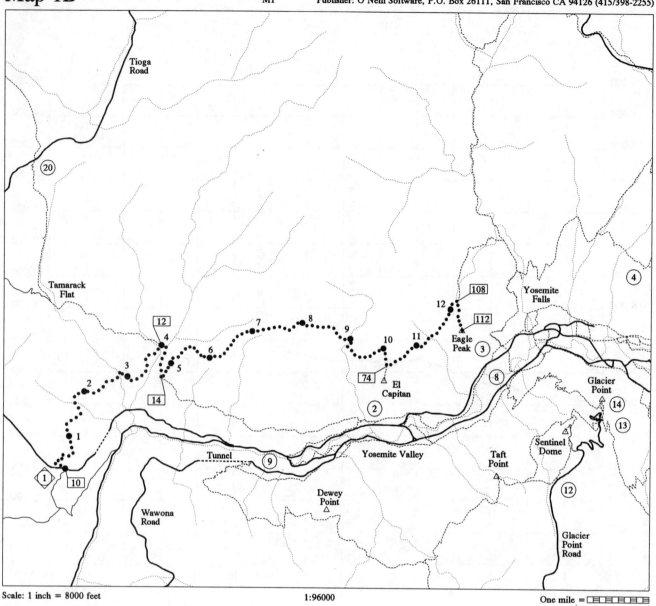

Scale: 1 inch = 8000 feet   1:96000   One mile =

Destination Chart

Num	Location	Elevation	Cumulative Distances				Incremental Distances			
			Miles	Up	Down	Total	Miles	Up	Down	Total
10	Big Oak Flat Road	4,760	0.0	0	0	0	0.0	0	0	0
12	Tamarack Creek Tr/Rockslide Rt	6,000	4.0	1,600	360	1,960	4.0	1,600	360	1,960
14	El Capitan Tr/Rockslide Rt	5,800	4.6	1,600	560	2,160	0.6	0	200	200
74	El Capitan Tr/Tr to El Capitan Top	7,600	10.3	3,800	960	4,760	5.7	2,200	400	2,600
108	Eagle Peak Tr/El Capitan Tr	7,360	12.2	4,080	1,480	5,560	1.9	280	520	800
112	Eagle Peak	7,779	12.8	4,539	1,520	6,059	0.6	459	40	499
	Totals		12.8	4,539	1,520	6,059	12.8	4,539	1,520	6,059

Publisher: O'Neill Software, P.O. Box 26111, San Francisco CA 94126 (415/398-2255)

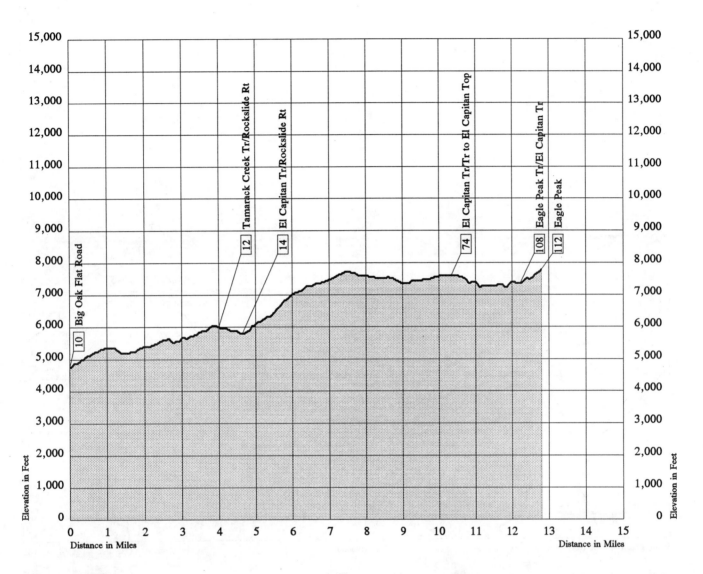

Mileage Chart

Mile	Elevation	Cumulative Distances			Incremental Distances		
		Up	Down	Rating	Up	Down	Rating
0	4,760	0	0	0	0	0	0
1	5,360	600	0	600	600	0	600
2	5,400	800	160	960	200	160	360
3	5,640	1,160	280	1,440	360	120	480
4	6,000	1,600	360	1,960	440	80	520
5	6,080	1,880	560	2,440	280	200	480
6	7,040	2,840	560	3,400	960	0	960
7	7,480	3,280	560	3,840	440	0	440
8	7,600	3,520	680	4,200	240	120	360
9	7,360	3,560	960	4,520	40	280	320
10	7,600	3,800	960	4,760	240	0	240
11	7,400	3,840	1,200	5,040	40	240	280
12	7,400	4,080	1,440	5,520	240	240	480
12.8	7,779	4,539	1,520	6,059	459	80	539
12.8	Totals	4,539	1,520	6,059	4,539	1,520	6,059

Notes

Route:

10 to 12:	Tamarack Creek Trail
12 to 14:	Rockslide Route
14 to 108:	El Capitan Trail
108 to 112:	Eagle Peak Trail

Trail from 108 to 112 not measured

Map Location

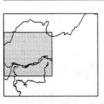

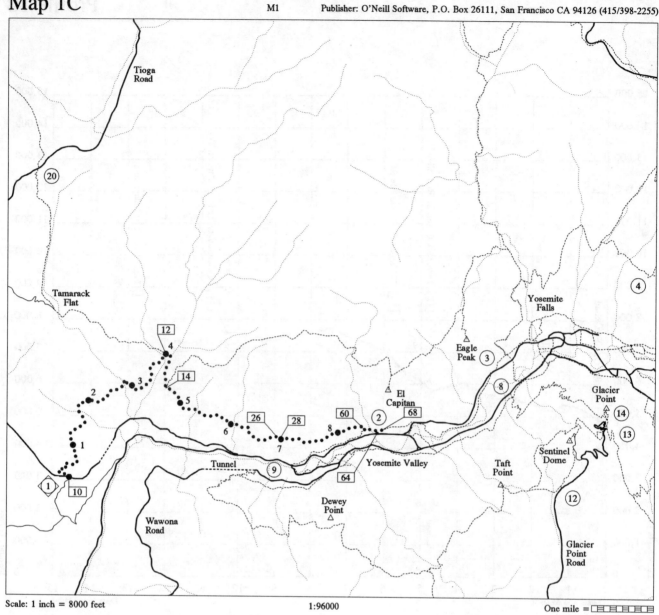

Scale: 1 inch = 8000 feet   1:96000   One mile =

Destination Chart

			Cumulative Distances				Incremental Distances			
Num	Location	Elevation	Miles	Up	Down	Total	Miles	Up	Down	Total
10	Big Oak Flat Road	4,760	0.0	0	0	0	0.0	0	0	0
12	Tamarack Creek Tr/Rockslide Rt	6,000	4.0	1,600	360	1,960	4.0	1,600	360	1,960
14	El Capitan Tr/Rockslide Rt	5,800	4.6	1,600	560	2,160	0.6	0	200	200
26	Slide Area Top - no trail	4,880	6.9	1,600	1,480	3,080	2.3	0	920	920
28	Slide Area Bottom - no trail	4,680	7.0	1,600	1,680	3,280	0.1	0	200	200
60	Rockslide Rt/Valley Tr	4,000	8.5	1,640	2,400	4,040	1.5	40	720	760
68	Valley Tr	3,960	8.8	1,640	2,440	4,080	0.3	0	40	40
64	Northside Drive	3,960	8.9	1,640	2,440	4,080	0.1	0	0	0
	Totals		8.9	1,640	2,440	4,080	8.9	1,640	2,440	4,080

Publisher: O'Neill Software, P.O. Box 26111, San Francisco CA 94126 (415/398-2255)

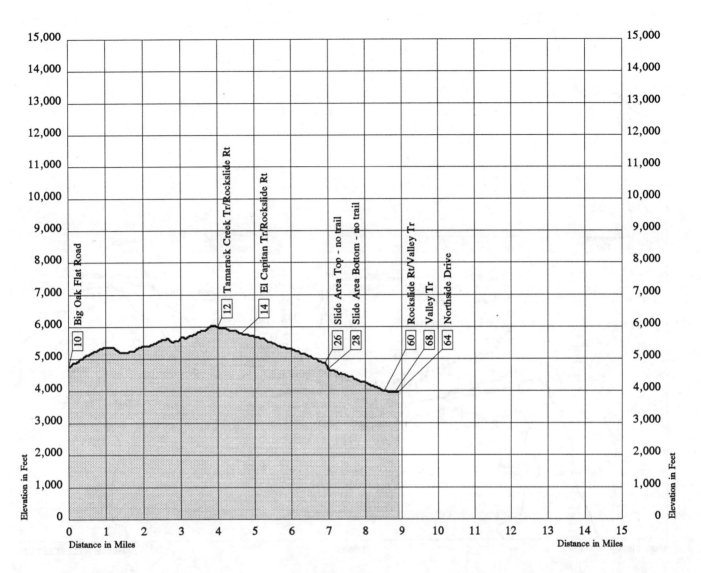

Mileage Chart

Mile	Elevation	Cumulative Distances			Incremental Distances		
		Up	Down	Rating	Up	Down	Rating
0	4,760	0	0	0	0	0	0
1	5,360	600	0	600	600	0	600
2	5,400	800	160	960	200	160	360
3	5,640	1,160	280	1,440	360	120	480
4	6,000	1,600	360	1,960	440	80	520
5	5,680	1,600	680	2,280	0	320	320
6	5,320	1,600	1,040	2,640	0	360	360
7	4,680	1,600	1,680	3,280	0	640	640
8	4,240	1,640	2,160	3,800	40	480	520
8.9	3,960	1,640	2,440	4,080	0	280	280
8.9	Totals	1,640	2,440	4,080	1,640	2,440	4,080

Notes

Route:
10 to 12:	Tamarack Creek Trail
12 to 60:	Rockslide Route
60 to 64:	Valley Trail

Trail from 14 to 64 not measured

Map Location

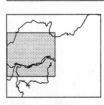

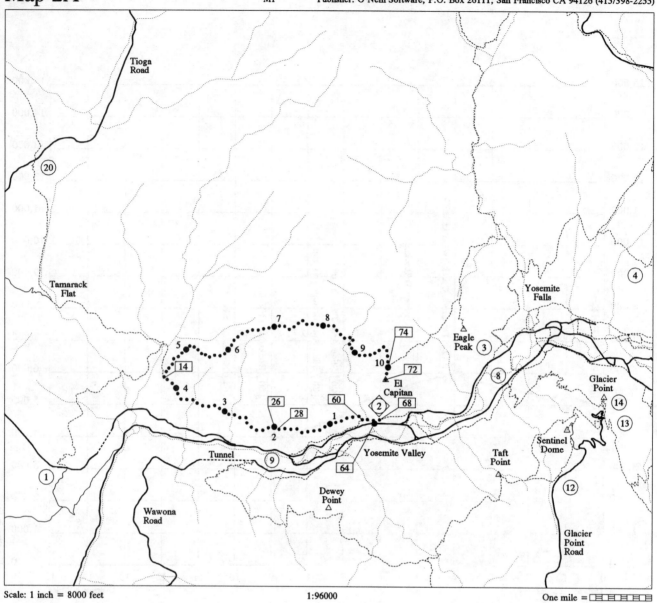

Scale: 1 inch = 8000 feet   1:96000   One mile =

Destination Chart

Num	Location	Elevation	Cumulative Distances				Incremental Distances			
			Miles	Up	Down	Total	Miles	Up	Down	Total
64	Northside Drive	3,960	0.0	0	0	0	0.0	0	0	0
68	Valley Tr	3,960	0.1	0	0	0	0.1	0	0	0
60	Rockslide Rt/Valley Tr	4,000	0.4	40	0	40	0.3	40	0	40
28	Slide Area Bottom - no trail	4,680	1.9	760	40	800	1.5	720	40	760
26	Slide Area Top - no trail	4,880	2.0	960	40	1,000	0.1	200	0	200
14	El Capitan Tr/Rockslide Rt	5,800	4.3	1,880	40	1,920	2.3	920	0	920
74	El Capitan Tr/Tr to El Capitan Top	7,600	10.0	4,080	440	4,520	5.7	2,200	400	2,600
72	El Capitan	7,569	10.2	4,089	480	4,569	0.2	9	40	49
		Totals	10.2	4,089	480	4,569	10.2	4,089	480	4,569

Publisher: O'Neill Software, P.O. Box 26111, San Francisco CA 94126 (415/398-2255)

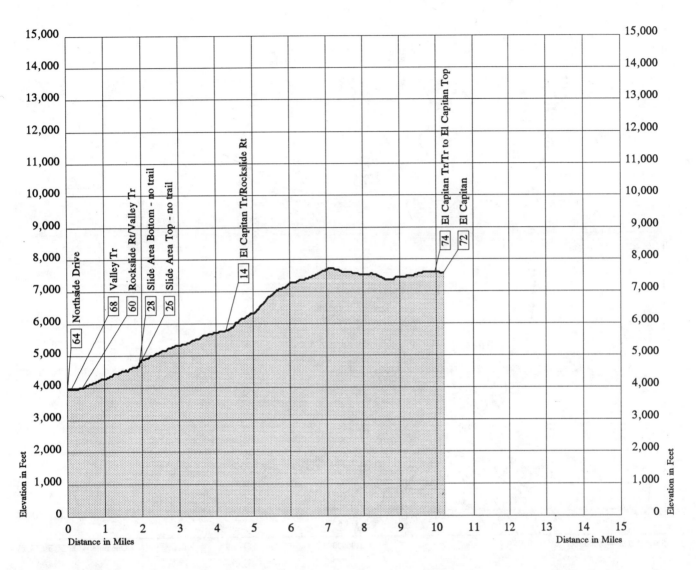

Mileage Chart

Mile	Elevation	Cumulative Distances			Incremental Distances		
		Up	Down	Rating	Up	Down	Rating
0	3,960	0	0	0	0	0	0
1	4,280	320	0	320	320	0	320
2	4,880	960	40	1,000	640	40	680
3	5,320	1,400	40	1,440	440	0	440
4	5,720	1,800	40	1,840	400	0	400
5	6,320	2,400	40	2,440	600	0	600
6	7,280	3,360	40	3,400	960	0	960
7	7,680	3,760	40	3,800	400	0	400
8	7,520	3,800	240	4,040	40	200	240
9	7,440	3,920	440	4,360	120	200	320
10	7,600	4,080	440	4,520	160	0	160
10.2	7,569	4,089	480	4,569	9	40	49
10.2	Totals	4,089	480	4,569	4,089	480	4,569

Notes

Route:

64 to 60:	Valley Trail
60 to 14:	Rockslide Route
14 to 74:	El Capitan Trail
74 to 72:	Trail to El Capitan Top

Trail from 64 to 14 not measured

Map Location

M2   Publisher: O'Neill Software, P.O. Box 26111, San Francisco CA 94126 (415/398-2255)

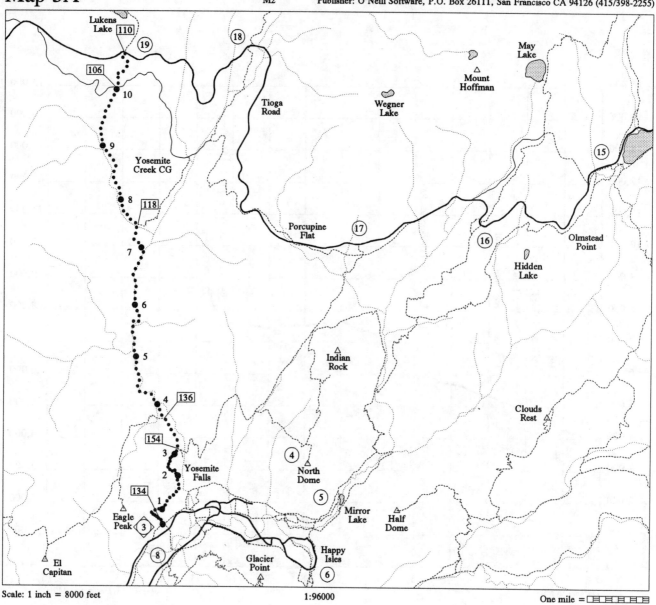

Scale: 1 inch = 8000 feet   1:96000   One mile = □□□□□□□

Destination Chart

Num	Location	Elevation	Cumulative Distances				Incremental Distances			
			Miles	Up	Down	Total	Miles	Up	Down	Total
134	Yosemite Falls Trailhead	4,000	0.0	0	0	0	0.0	0	0	0
154	Yosemite Falls Tr/North Dome Tr	6,640	3.2	2,840	200	3,040	3.2	2,840	200	3,040
136	El Capitan Tr/Yosemite Creek Tr	6,840	3.7	3,120	280	3,400	0.5	280	80	360
118	Yosemite Creek Tr/Hetch Hetchy Tr	7,160	7.4	3,480	320	3,800	3.7	360	40	400
106	Hetch Hetchy Tr/Old Tioga Rd	7,960	10.0	4,280	320	4,600	2.6	800	0	800
110	Tioga Road	8,160	10.8	4,480	320	4,800	0.8	200	0	200
	Totals		10.8	4,480	320	4,800	10.8	4,480	320	4,800

Yosemite Falls Trailhead to Tioga Road   3A

Publisher: O'Neill Software, P.O. Box 26111, San Francisco CA 94126 (415/398-2255)

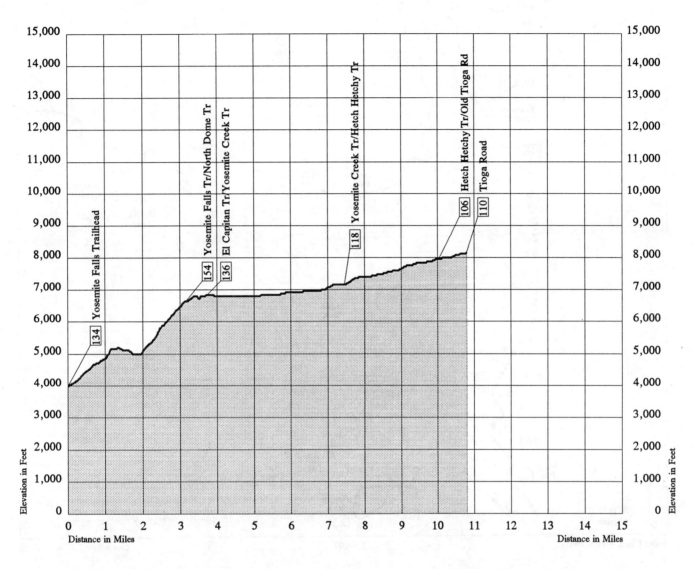

Mileage Chart

Mile	Elevation	Cumulative Distances			Incremental Distances		
		Up	Down	Rating	Up	Down	Rating
0	4,000	0	0	0	0	0	0
1	4,880	880	0	880	880	0	880
2	5,080	1,280	200	1,480	400	200	600
3	6,480	2,680	200	2,880	1,400	0	1,400
4	6,800	3,120	320	3,440	440	120	560
5	6,800	3,120	320	3,440	0	0	0
6	6,920	3,240	320	3,560	120	0	120
7	7,080	3,400	320	3,720	160	0	160
8	7,400	3,720	320	4,040	320	0	320
9	7,640	3,960	320	4,280	240	0	240
10	7,960	4,280	320	4,600	320	0	320
10.8	8,160	4,480	320	4,800	200	0	200
10.8	Totals	4,480	320	4,800	4,480	320	4,800

Notes

Route:
134 to 154:	Yosemite Falls Trail
154 to 118:	Yosemite Creek Trail
118 to 110:	Hetch Hetchy Trail

Trail from 106 to 110 not measured
See 19A for opposite direction

Map Location

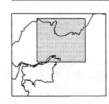

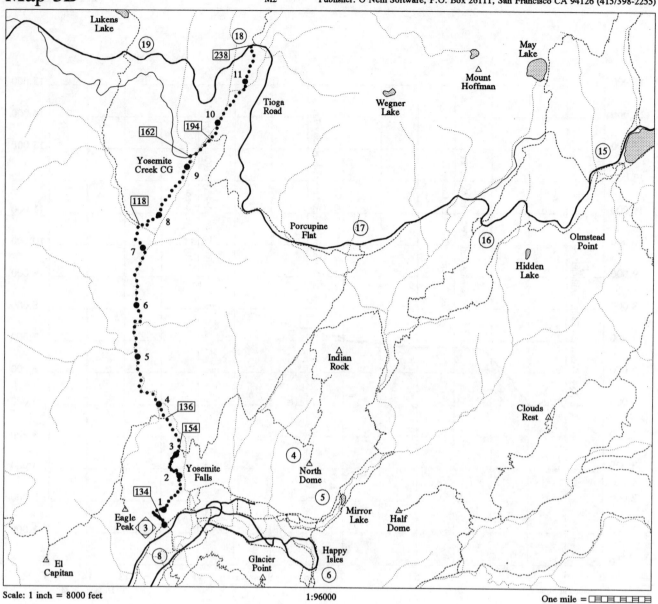

Scale: 1 inch = 8000 feet   1:96000   One mile = ⬚⬚⬚⬚⬚⬚

Destination Chart

Num	Location	Elevation	Cumulative Distances				Incremental Distances			
			Miles	Up	Down	Total	Miles	Up	Down	Total
134	Yosemite Falls Trailhead	4,000	0.0	0	0	0	0.0	0	0	0
154	Yosemite Falls Tr/North Dome Tr	6,640	3.2	2,840	200	3,040	3.2	2,840	200	3,040
136	El Capitan Tr/Yosemite Creek Tr	6,840	3.7	3,120	280	3,400	0.5	280	80	360
118	Yosemite Creek Tr/Hetch Hetchy Tr	7,160	7.4	3,480	320	3,800	3.7	360	40	400
162	Yosemite Creek Campground	7,160	9.2	3,640	480	4,120	1.8	160	160	320
194	Yosemite Creek Tr/Old Tioga Rd	7,200	9.6	3,680	480	4,160	0.4	40	0	40
238	Yosemite Creek Trailhead	7,480	11.7	3,960	480	4,440	2.1	280	0	280
	Totals		11.7	3,960	480	4,440	11.7	3,960	480	4,440

Yosemite Falls Trailhead to Yosemite Creek Trailhead

3B

Publisher: O'Neill Software, P.O. Box 26111, San Francisco CA 94126 (415/398-2255)

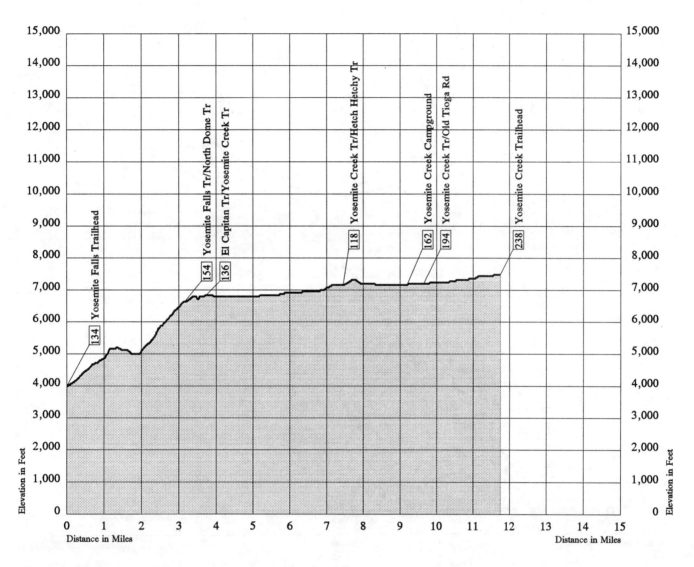

Mileage Chart

Mile	Elevation	Cumulative Distances			Incremental Distances		
		Up	Down	Rating	Up	Down	Rating
0	4,000	0	0	0	0	0	0
1	4,880	880	0	880	880	0	880
2	5,080	1,280	200	1,480	400	200	600
3	6,480	2,680	200	2,880	1,400	0	1,400
4	6,800	3,120	320	3,440	440	120	560
5	6,800	3,120	320	3,440	0	0	0
6	6,920	3,240	320	3,560	120	0	120
7	7,080	3,400	320	3,720	160	0	160
8	7,200	3,640	440	4,080	240	120	360
9	7,160	3,640	480	4,120	0	40	40
10	7,240	3,720	480	4,200	80	0	80
11	7,360	3,840	480	4,320	120	0	120
11.7	7,480	3,960	480	4,440	120	0	120
11.7	Totals	3,960	480	4,440	3,960	480	4,440

Notes

Route:

134 to 154:	Yosemite Falls Trail
154 to 162:	Yosemite Creek Trail
162 to 194:	Old Tioga Road
194 to 238:	Yosemite Creek Trail

See 18A for opposite direction

Map Location

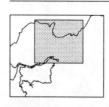

Yosemite Falls Trailhead to Yosemite Creek Trailhead

M2   Publisher: O'Neill Software, P.O. Box 26111, San Francisco CA 94126 (415/398-2255)

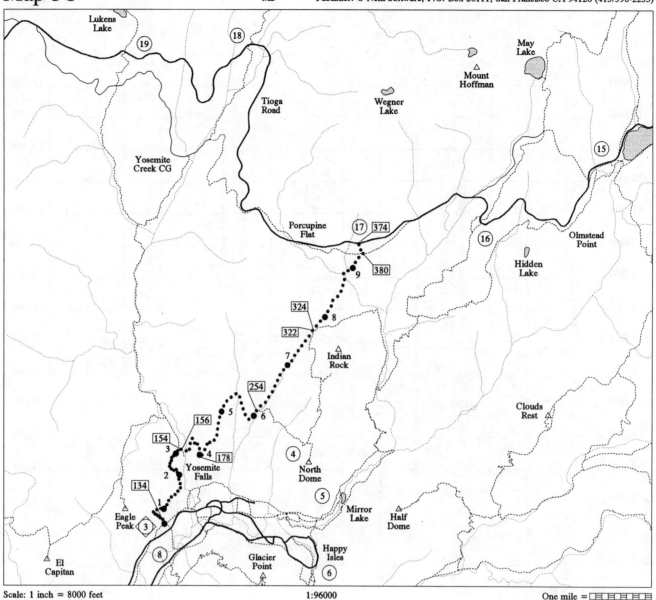

Scale: 1 inch = 8000 feet   1:96000   One mile = ▨▨▨▨▨▨

Destination Chart

Num	Location	Elevation	Cumulative Distances				Incremental Distances			
			Miles	Up	Down	Total	Miles	Up	Down	Total
134	Yosemite Falls Trailhead	4,000	0.0	0	0	0	0.0	0	0	0
154	Yosemite Falls Tr/North Dome Tr	6,640	3.2	2,840	200	3,040	3.2	2,840	200	3,040
156	North Dome Tr/Tr to Yosemite Falls	6,680	3.2	2,880	200	3,080	0.0	40	0	40
178	Yosemite Point	7,000	4.1	3,280	280	3,560	0.9	400	80	480
254	North Dome Tr/Lehamite Tr	7,000	6.1	3,720	720	4,440	2.0	440	440	880
322	Indian Ridge Tr/Lehamite Tr	7,840	7.7	4,560	720	5,280	1.6	840	0	840
324	Indian Ridge Tr/Porcupine Creek Tr	7,840	7.7	4,560	720	5,280	0.0	0	0	0
380	Porcupine Creek Tr/Old Tioga Rd	7,960	9.3	4,720	760	5,480	1.6	160	40	200
374	Porcupine Creek Trailhead	8,120	9.5	4,880	760	5,640	0.2	160	0	160
	Totals		9.5	4,880	760	5,640	9.5	4,880	760	5,640

Yosemite Falls Trailhead to Porcupine Creek Trailhead   3C

Publisher: O'Neill Software, P.O. Box 26111, San Francisco CA 94126 (415/398-2255)

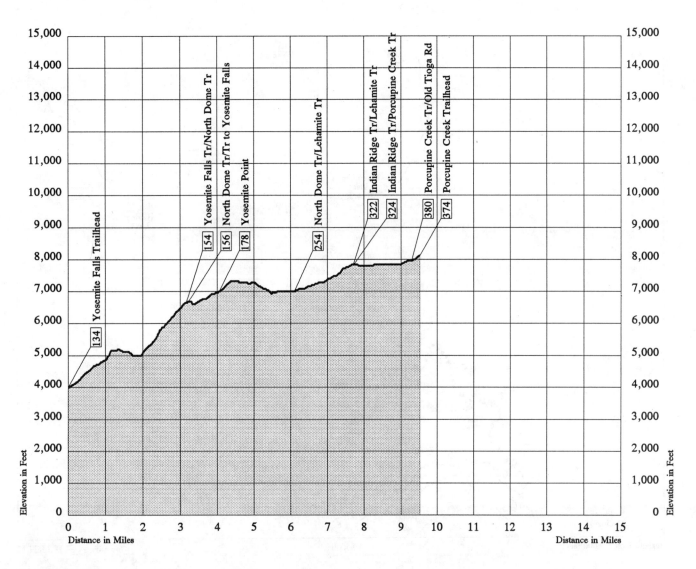

Mileage Chart

Mile	Elevation	Cumulative Distances			Incremental Distances		
		Up	Down	Rating	Up	Down	Rating
0	4,000	0	0	0	0	0	0
1	4,880	880	0	880	880	0	880
2	5,080	1,280	200	1,480	400	200	600
3	6,480	2,680	200	2,880	1,400	0	1,400
4	6,960	3,240	280	3,520	560	80	640
5	7,280	3,640	360	4,000	400	80	480
6	7,000	3,720	720	4,440	80	360	440
7	7,360	4,080	720	4,800	360	0	360
8	7,800	4,560	760	5,320	480	40	520
9	7,840	4,600	760	5,360	40	0	40
9.5	8,120	4,880	760	5,640	280	0	280
9.5	Totals	4,880	760	5,640	4,880	760	5,640

Notes

Route:

134 to 154:	Yosemite Falls Trail
154 to 254:	North Dome Trail
254 to 324:	Lehamite Trail
324 to 374:	Porcupine Creek Trail

Trail from 254 to 322 not measured
See 17A for opposite direction

Map Location

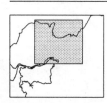

Yosemite Falls Trailhead to Porcupine Creek Trailhead

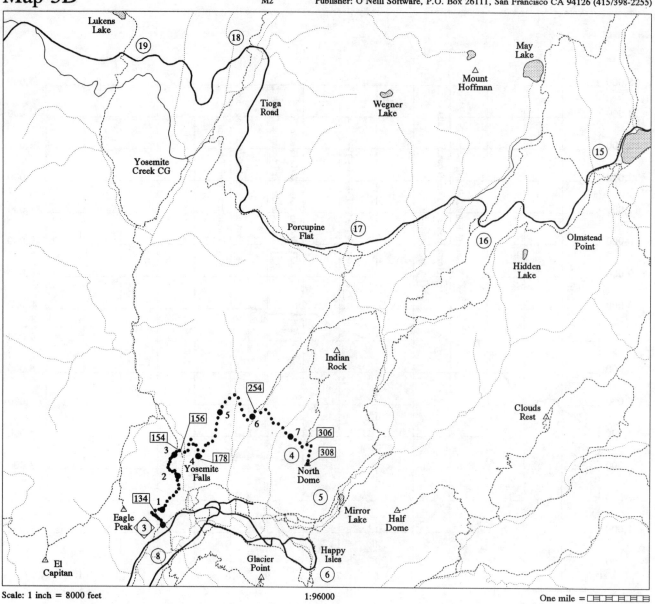

Scale: 1 inch = 8000 feet   1:96000   One mile = ▭▭▭▭▭▭

Destination Chart

Num	Location	Elevation	Cumulative Distances				Incremental Distances			
			Miles	Up	Down	Total	Miles	Up	Down	Total
134	Yosemite Falls Trailhead	4,000	0.0	0	0	0	0.0	0	0	0
154	Yosemite Falls Tr/North Dome Tr	6,640	3.2	2,840	200	3,040	3.2	2,840	200	3,040
156	North Dome Tr/Tr to Yosemite Falls	6,680	3.2	2,880	200	3,080	0.0	40	0	40
178	Yosemite Point	7,000	4.1	3,280	280	3,560	0.9	400	80	480
254	North Dome Tr/Lehamite Tr	7,000	6.1	3,720	720	4,440	2.0	440	440	880
306	North Dome Tr/Indian Ridge Tr	7,560	7.4	4,400	840	5,240	1.3	680	120	800
308	North Dome	7,542	7.9	4,542	1,000	5,542	0.5	142	160	302
		Totals	7.9	4,542	1,000	5,542	7.9	4,542	1,000	5,542

Yosemite Falls Trailhead to North Dome

3D

Publisher: O'Neill Software, P.O. Box 26111, San Francisco CA 94126 (415/398-2255)

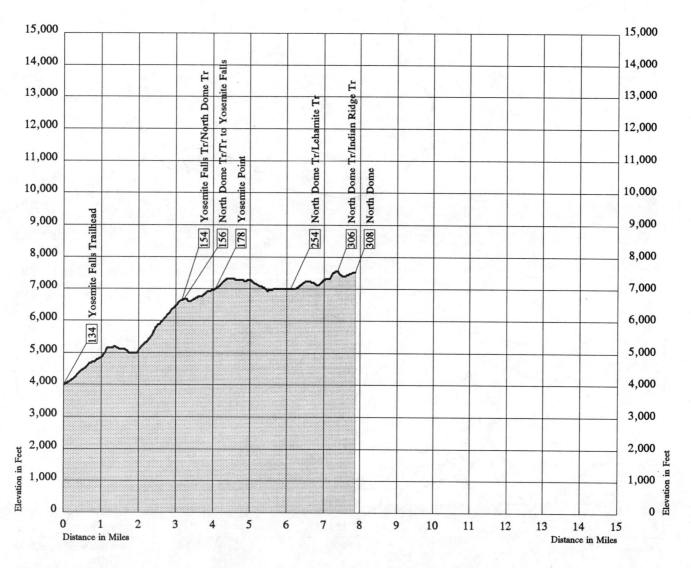

Mileage Chart

Mile	Elevation	Cumulative Distances			Incremental Distances		
		Up	Down	Rating	Up	Down	Rating
0	4,000	0	0	0	0	0	0
1	4,880	880	0	880	880	0	880
2	5,080	1,280	200	1,480	400	200	600
3	6,480	2,680	200	2,880	1,400	0	1,400
4	6,960	3,240	280	3,520	560	80	640
5	7,280	3,640	360	4,000	400	80	480
6	7,000	3,720	720	4,440	80	360	440
7	7,280	4,120	840	4,960	400	120	520
7.9	7,542	4,542	1,000	5,542	422	160	582
7.9	Totals	4,542	1,000	5,542	4,542	1,000	5,542

Notes

Route:

134 to 154: Yosemite Falls Trail
154 to 308: North Dome Trail

Map Location

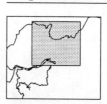

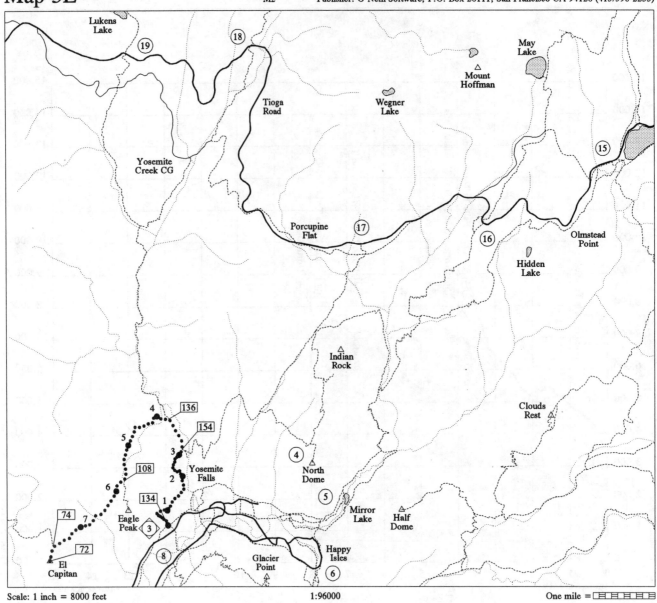

Scale: 1 inch = 8000 feet   1:96000   One mile =

Destination Chart

Num	Location	Elevation	Cumulative Distances				Incremental Distances			
			Miles	Up	Down	Total	Miles	Up	Down	Total
134	Yosemite Falls Trailhead	4,000	0.0	0	0	0	0.0	0	0	0
154	Yosemite Falls Tr/North Dome Tr	6,640	3.2	2,840	200	3,040	3.2	2,840	200	3,040
136	El Capitan Tr/Yosemite Creek Tr	6,840	3.7	3,120	280	3,400	0.5	280	80	360
108	Eagle Peak Tr/El Capitan Tr	7,360	5.7	3,640	280	3,920	2.0	520	0	520
74	El Capitan Tr/Tr to El Capitan Top	7,600	7.6	4,160	560	4,720	1.9	520	280	800
72	El Capitan	7,569	7.9	4,169	600	4,769	0.3	9	40	49
		Totals	7.9	4,169	600	4,769	7.9	4,169	600	4,769

Publisher: O'Neill Software, P.O. Box 26111, San Francisco CA 94126 (415/398-2255)

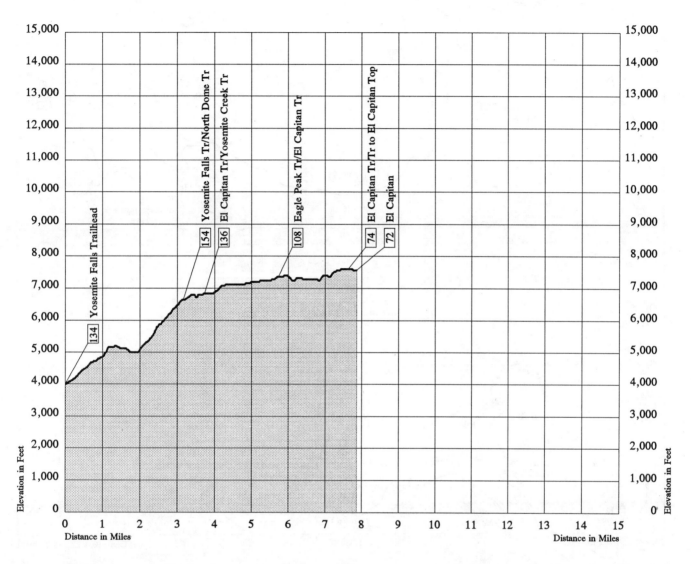

Mileage Chart

		Cumulative Distances			Incremental Distances		
Mile	Elevation	Up	Down	Rating	Up	Down	Rating
0	4,000	0	0	0	0	0	0
1	4,880	880	0	880	880	0	880
2	5,080	1,280	200	1,480	400	200	600
3	6,480	2,680	200	2,880	1,400	0	1,400
4	6,880	3,160	280	3,440	480	80	560
5	7,200	3,480	280	3,760	320	0	320
6	7,360	3,680	320	4,000	200	40	240
7	7,400	3,920	520	4,440	240	200	440
7.9	7,569	4,169	600	4,769	249	80	329
7.9	Totals	4,169	600	4,769	4,169	600	4,769

Notes

Route:

134 to 154:	Yosemite Falls Trail
154 to 136:	Yosemite Creek Trail
136 to 74:	El Capitan Trail
74 to 72:	Trail to El Capitan Top

Map Location

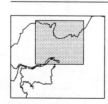

Yosemite Falls Trailhead to El Capitan

M2   Publisher: O'Neill Software, P.O. Box 26111, San Francisco CA 94126 (415/398-2255)

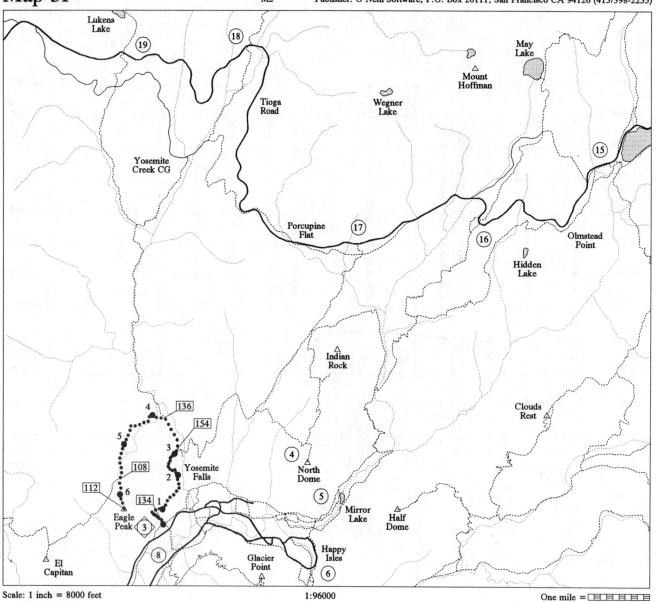

Scale: 1 inch = 8000 feet   1:96000   One mile = ▣▣▣▣▣▣

Destination Chart

Num	Location	Elevation	Cumulative Distances				Incremental Distances			
			Miles	Up	Down	Total	Miles	Up	Down	Total
134	Yosemite Falls Trailhead	4,000	0.0	0	0	0	0.0	0	0	0
154	Yosemite Falls Tr/North Dome Tr	6,640	3.2	2,840	200	3,040	3.2	2,840	200	3,040
136	El Capitan Tr/Yosemite Creek Tr	6,840	3.7	3,120	280	3,400	0.5	280	80	360
108	Eagle Peak Tr/El Capitan Tr	7,360	5.7	3,640	280	3,920	2.0	520	0	520
112	Eagle Peak	7,779	6.3	4,099	320	4,419	0.6	459	40	499
		Totals	6.3	4,099	320	4,419	6.3	4,099	320	4,419

Yosemite Falls Trailhead to Eagle Peak

Publisher: O'Neill Software, P.O. Box 26111, San Francisco CA 94126 (415/398-2255)

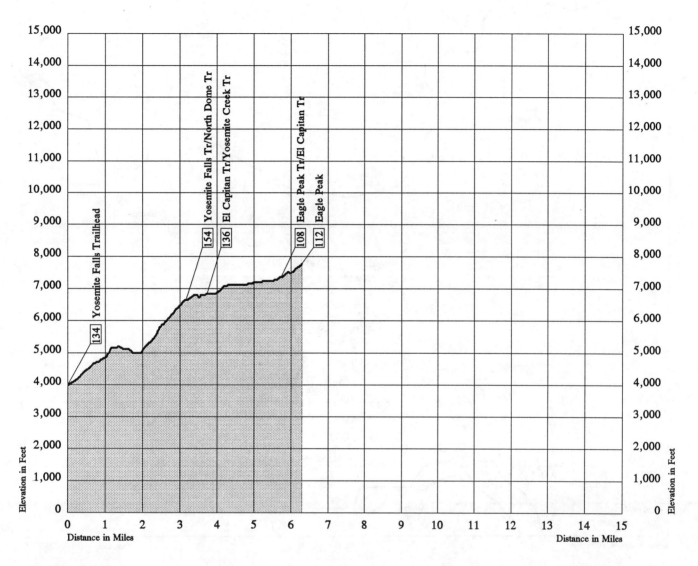

Mileage Chart

Mile	Elevation	Cumulative Distances			Incremental Distances		
		Up	Down	Rating	Up	Down	Rating
0	4,000	0	0	0	0	0	0
1	4,880	880	0	880	880	0	880
2	5,080	1,280	200	1,480	400	200	600
3	6,480	2,680	200	2,880	1,400	0	1,400
4	6,880	3,160	280	3,440	480	80	560
5	7,200	3,480	280	3,760	320	0	320
6	7,520	3,840	320	4,160	360	40	400
6.3	7,779	4,099	320	4,419	259	0	259
6.3	Totals	4,099	320	4,419	4,099	320	4,419

Notes

Route:

134 to 154:	Yosemite Falls Trail
154 to 136:	Yosemite Creek Trail
136 to 108:	El Capitan Trail
108 to 112:	Eagle Peak Trail

Trail from 108 to 112 not measured

Map Location

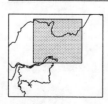

Yosemite Falls Trailhead to Eagle Peak

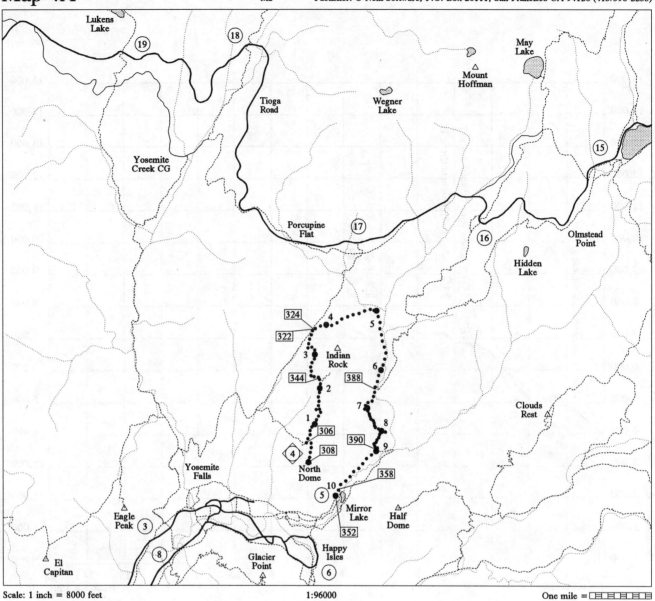

Scale: 1 inch = 8000 feet   1:96000   One mile =

Destination Chart

			Cumulative Distances				Incremental Distances			
Num	Location	Elevation	Miles	Up	Down	Total	Miles	Up	Down	Total
308	North Dome	7,542	0.0	0	0	0	0.0	0	0	0
306	North Dome Tr/Indian Ridge Tr	7,560	0.5	160	142	302	0.5	160	142	302
344	Indian Ridge Tr/Natural Arch Tr	8,120	2.2	760	182	942	1.7	600	40	640
322	Indian Ridge Tr/Lehamite Tr	7,840	3.7	840	542	1,382	1.5	80	360	440
324	Indian Ridge Tr/Porcupine Creek Tr	7,840	3.7	840	542	1,382	0.0	0	0	0
388	Snow Creek Tr/Indian Ridge Tr	6,720	6.3	840	1,662	2,502	2.6	0	1,120	1,120
390	Snow Creek Tr/Mirror Mdw Tr	4,120	9.0	840	4,262	5,102	2.7	0	2,600	2,600
358	Mirror Mdw Tr/Mirror Lake Tr	4,120	9.9	840	4,262	5,102	0.9	0	0	0
352	Mirror Lake Trailhead	4,120	10.0	840	4,262	5,102	0.1	0	0	0
	Totals		10.0	840	4,262	5,102	10.0	840	4,262	5,102

North Dome to Mirror Lake Trailhead   4A

Publisher: O'Neill Software, P.O. Box 26111, San Francisco CA 94126 (415/398-2255)

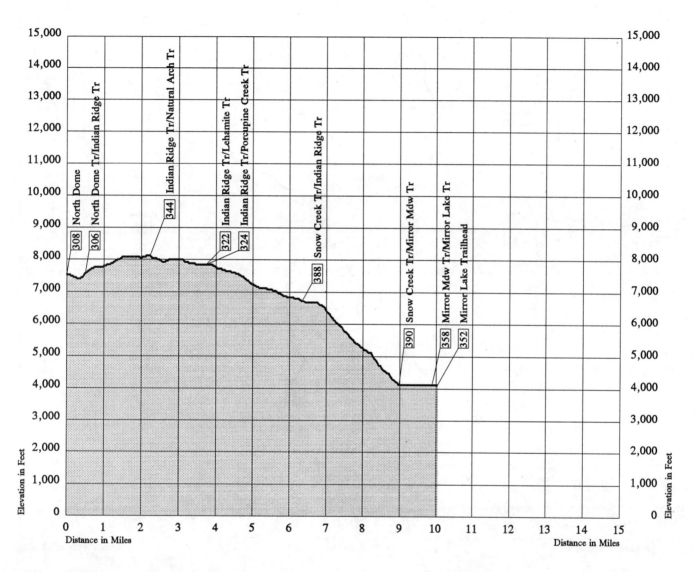

Mileage Chart

Mile	Elevation	Cumulative Distances			Incremental Distances		
		Up	Down	Rating	Up	Down	Rating
0	7,542	0	0	0	0	0	0
1	7,800	400	142	542	400	142	542
2	8,040	680	182	862	280	40	320
3	8,000	840	382	1,222	160	200	360
4	7,760	840	622	1,462	0	240	240
5	7,240	840	1,142	1,982	0	520	520
6	6,840	840	1,542	2,382	0	400	400
7	6,400	840	1,982	2,822	0	440	440
8	5,240	840	3,142	3,982	0	1,160	1,160
9	4,120	840	4,262	5,102	0	1,120	1,120
10	4,120	840	4,262	5,102	0	0	0
10.0	Totals	840	4,262	5,102	840	4,262	5,102

Notes

Route:

308 to 306:	North Dome Trail
306 to 388:	Indian Ridge Trail
388 to 390:	Snow Creek Trail
390 to 352:	Mirror Meadow Trail

See 5D for opposite direction

Map Location

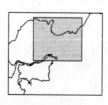

North Dome to Mirror Lake Trailhead

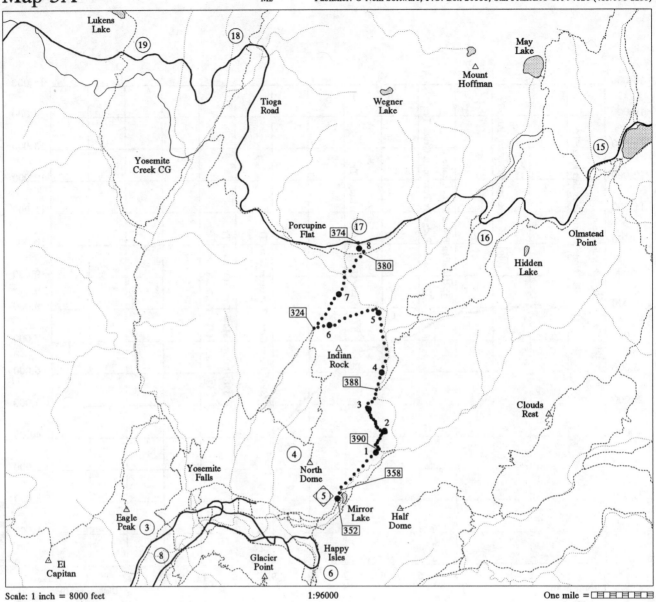

Scale: 1 inch = 8000 feet   1:96000   One mile =

Destination Chart

Num	Location	Elevation	Cumulative Distances				Incremental Distances			
			Miles	Up	Down	Total	Miles	Up	Down	Total
352	Mirror Lake Trailhead	4,120	0.0	0	0	0	0.0	0	0	0
358	Mirror Mdw Tr/Mirror Lake Tr	4,120	0.2	0	0	0	0.2	0	0	0
390	Snow Creek Tr/Mirror Mdw Tr	4,120	1.1	0	0	0	0.9	0	0	0
388	Snow Creek Tr/Indian Ridge Tr	6,720	3.7	2,600	0	2,600	2.6	2,600	0	2,600
324	Indian Ridge Tr/Porcupine Creek Tr	7,840	6.3	3,720	0	3,720	2.6	1,120	0	1,120
380	Porcupine Creek Tr/Old Tioga Rd	7,960	7.9	3,880	40	3,920	1.6	160	40	200
374	Porcupine Creek Trailhead	8,120	8.1	4,040	40	4,080	0.2	160	0	160
	Totals		8.1	4,040	40	4,080	8.1	4,040	40	4,080

Mirror Lake Trailhead to Porcupine Creek Trailhead   5A

Publisher: O'Neill Software, P.O. Box 26111, San Francisco CA 94126 (415/398-2255)

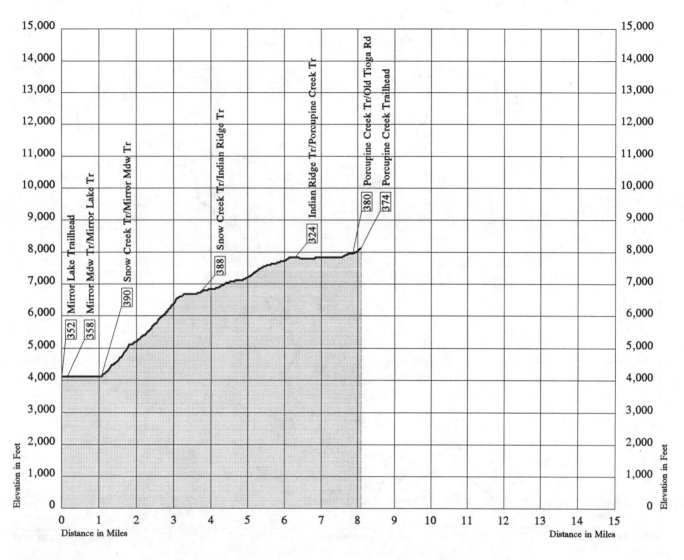

Mileage Chart

Mile	Elevation	Cumulative Distances			Incremental Distances		
		Up	Down	Rating	Up	Down	Rating
0	4,120	0	0	0	0	0	0
1	4,120	0	0	0	0	0	0
2	5,200	1,080	0	1,080	1,080	0	1,080
3	6,360	2,240	0	2,240	1,160	0	1,160
4	6,840	2,720	0	2,720	480	0	480
5	7,200	3,080	0	3,080	360	0	360
6	7,720	3,600	0	3,600	520	0	520
7	7,840	3,760	40	3,800	160	40	200
8	8,040	3,960	40	4,000	200	0	200
8.1	8,120	4,040	40	4,080	80	0	80
8.1	Totals	4,040	40	4,080	4,040	40	4,080

Notes

Route:

352 to 390:	Mirror Meadow Trail
390 to 388:	Snow Creek Trail
388 to 324:	Indian Ridge Trail
324 to 374:	Porcupine Creek Trail

See 17B for opposite direction

Map Location

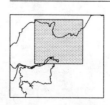

Mirror Lake Trailhead to Porcupine Creek Trailhead

M2   Publisher: O'Neill Software, P.O. Box 26111, San Francisco CA 94126 (415/398-2255)

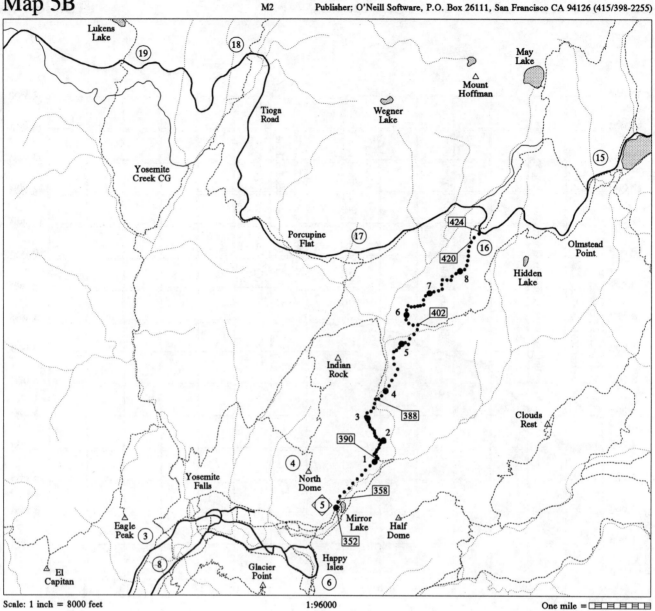

Scale: 1 inch = 8000 feet   1:96000   One mile = ▨▨▨▨▨

Destination Chart

Num	Location	Elevation	Cumulative Distances				Incremental Distances			
			Miles	Up	Down	Total	Miles	Up	Down	Total
352	Mirror Lake Trailhead	4,120	0.0	0	0	0	0.0	0	0	0
358	Mirror Mdw Tr/Mirror Lake Tr	4,120	0.2	0	0	0	0.2	0	0	0
390	Snow Creek Tr/Mirror Mdw Tr	4,120	1.1	0	0	0	0.9	0	0	0
388	Snow Creek Tr/Indian Ridge Tr	6,720	3.7	2,600	0	2,600	2.6	2,600	0	2,600
402	Snow Creek Tr/Tenaya Lake Tr	7,680	5.6	3,600	40	3,640	1.9	1,000	40	1,040
420	Snow Creek Tr/Quarry Tr	8,600	8.7	4,520	40	4,560	3.1	920	0	920
424	Snow Creek Trailhead	8,560	8.9	4,520	80	4,600	0.2	0	40	40
	Totals		8.9	4,520	80	4,600	8.9	4,520	80	4,600

Mirror Lake Trailhead to Snow Creek Trailhead   5B

Publisher: O'Neill Software, P.O. Box 26111, San Francisco CA 94126 (415/398-2255)

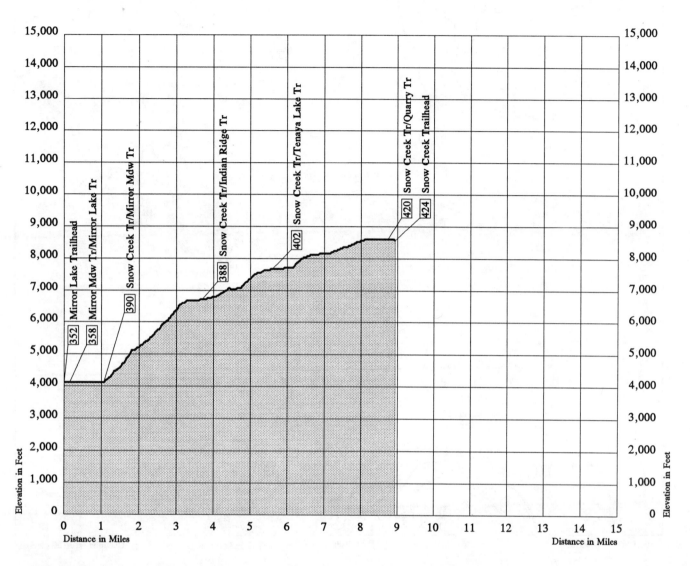

Mileage Chart

		Cumulative Distances			Incremental Distances		
Mile	Elevation	Up	Down	Rating	Up	Down	Rating
0	4,120	0	0	0	0	0	0
1	4,120	0	0	0	0	0	0
2	5,200	1,080	0	1,080	1,080	0	1,080
3	6,360	2,240	0	2,240	1,160	0	1,160
4	6,800	2,680	0	2,680	440	0	440
5	7,360	3,280	40	3,320	600	40	640
6	7,720	3,640	40	3,680	360	0	360
7	8,160	4,080	40	4,120	440	0	440
8	8,560	4,480	40	4,520	400	0	400
8.9	8,560	4,520	80	4,600	40	40	80
8.9	Totals	4,520	80	4,600	4,520	80	4,600

Notes

Route:

352 to 390:	Mirror Meadow Trail
390 to 424:	Snow Creek Trail

See 16A for opposite direction

Map Location

M2   Publisher: O'Neill Software, P.O. Box 26111, San Francisco CA 94126 (415/398-2255)

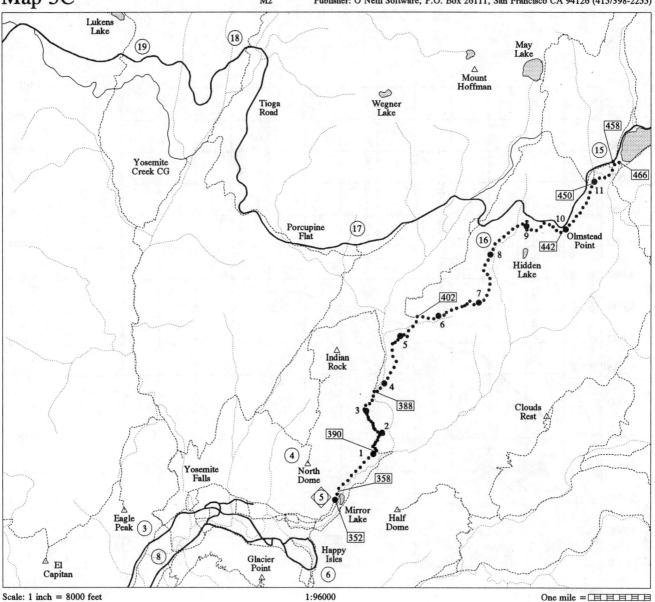

Scale: 1 inch = 8000 feet   1:96000   One mile =

Destination Chart

Num	Location	Elevation	Cumulative Distances				Incremental Distances			
			Miles	Up	Down	Total	Miles	Up	Down	Total
352	Mirror Lake Trailhead	4,120	0.0	0	0	0	0.0	0	0	0
358	Mirror Mdw Tr/Mirror Lake Tr	4,120	0.2	0	0	0	0.2	0	0	0
390	Snow Creek Tr/Mirror Mdw Tr	4,120	1.1	0	0	0	0.9	0	0	0
388	Snow Creek Tr/Indian Ridge Tr	6,720	3.7	2,600	0	2,600	2.6	2,600	0	2,600
402	Snow Creek Tr/Tenaya Lake Tr	7,680	5.6	3,600	40	3,640	1.9	1,000	40	1,040
442	Olmstead Point	8,360	9.9	4,680	440	5,120	4.3	1,080	400	1,480
450	Tenaya Lake Tr/Tr to Tioga Road	8,200	11.0	4,680	600	5,280	1.1	0	160	160
466	Tenaya Lake CG	8,160	11.6	4,680	640	5,320	0.6	0	40	40
458	Tenaya Lake Trailhead	8,200	11.7	4,720	640	5,360	0.1	40	0	40
		Totals	11.7	4,720	640	5,360	11.7	4,720	640	5,360

Mirror Lake Trailhead to Tenaya Lake Trailhead   5C

Publisher: O'Neill Software, P.O. Box 26111, San Francisco CA 94126 (415/398-2255)

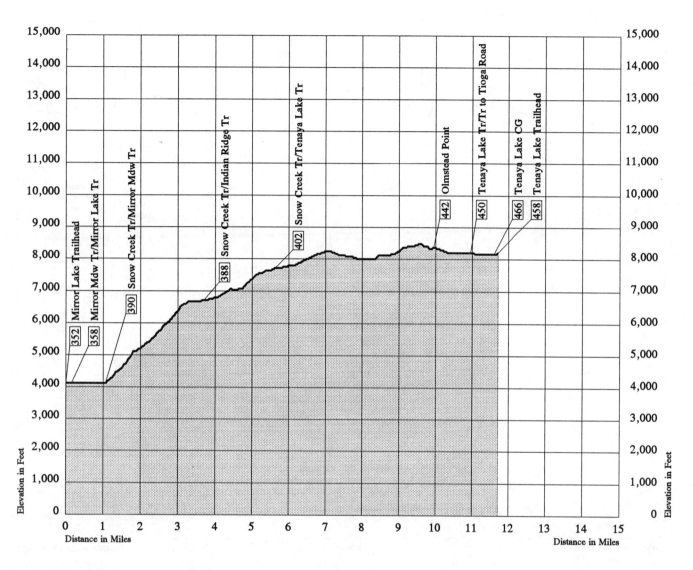

Mileage Chart

Mile	Elevation	Cumulative Distances			Incremental Distances		
		Up	Down	Rating	Up	Down	Rating
0	4,120	0	0	0	0	0	0
1	4,120	0	0	0	0	0	0
2	5,200	1,080	0	1,080	1,080	0	1,080
3	6,360	2,240	0	2,240	1,160	0	1,160
4	6,800	2,680	0	2,680	440	0	440
5	7,360	3,280	40	3,320	600	40	640
6	7,800	3,720	40	3,760	440	0	440
7	8,240	4,160	40	4,200	440	0	440
8	8,000	4,160	280	4,440	0	240	240
9	8,240	4,400	280	4,680	240	0	240
10	8,360	4,680	440	5,120	280	160	440
11	8,200	4,680	600	5,280	0	160	160
11.7	8,200	4,720	640	5,360	40	40	80
11.7	Totals	4,720	640	5,360	4,720	640	5,360

Notes

Route:
352 to 390: Mirror Meadow Trail
390 to 402: Snow Creek Trail
402 to 458: Tenaya Lake Trail

See 15A for opposite direction

Map Location

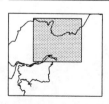

Mirror Lake Trailhead to Tenaya Lake Trailhead

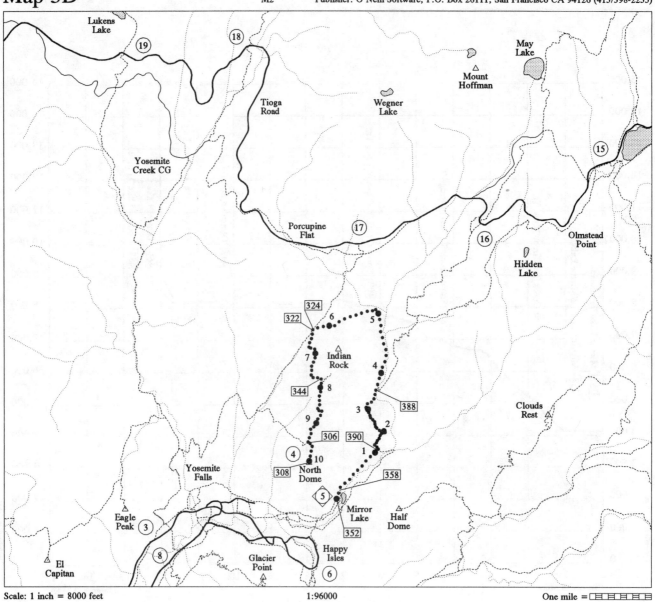

Scale: 1 inch = 8000 feet   1:96000   One mile = ▯▯▯▯▯▯

Destination Chart

Num	Location	Elevation	Cumulative Distances				Incremental Distances			
			Miles	Up	Down	Total	Miles	Up	Down	Total
352	Mirror Lake Trailhead	4,120	0.0	0	0	0	0.0	0	0	0
358	Mirror Mdw Tr/Mirror Lake Tr	4,120	0.2	0	0	0	0.2	0	0	0
390	Snow Creek Tr/Mirror Mdw Tr	4,120	1.1	0	0	0	0.9	0	0	0
388	Snow Creek Tr/Indian Ridge Tr	6,720	3.7	2,600	0	2,600	2.6	2,600	0	2,600
324	Indian Ridge Tr/Porcupine Creek Tr	7,840	6.3	3,720	0	3,720	2.6	1,120	0	1,120
322	Indian Ridge Tr/Lehamite Tr	7,840	6.3	3,720	0	3,720	0.0	0	0	0
344	Indian Ridge Tr/Natural Arch Tr	8,120	7.8	4,080	80	4,160	1.5	360	80	440
306	North Dome Tr/Indian Ridge Tr	7,560	9.5	4,120	680	4,800	1.7	40	600	640
308	North Dome	7,542	10.0	4,262	840	5,102	0.5	142	160	302
		Totals	10.0	4,262	840	5,102	10.0	4,262	840	5,102

Mirror Lake Trailhead to North Dome

5D

Publisher: O'Neill Software, P.O. Box 26111, San Francisco CA 94126 (415/398-2255)

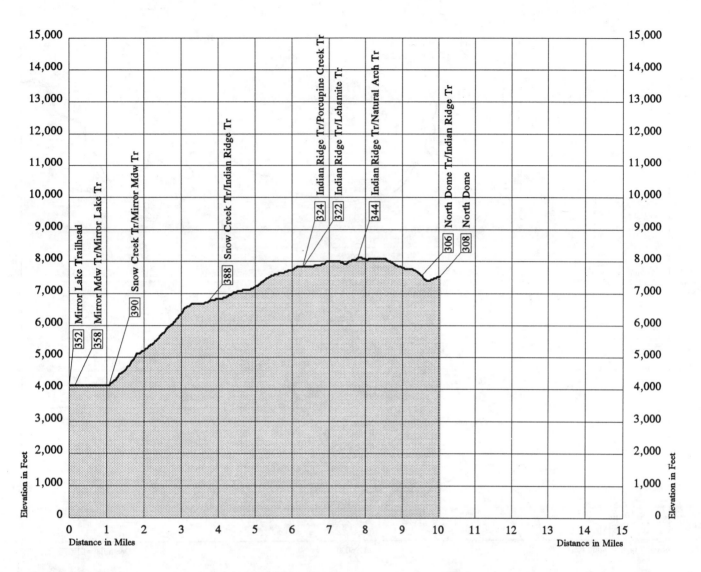

Mileage Chart

Mile	Elevation	Cumulative Distances			Incremental Distances		
		Up	Down	Rating	Up	Down	Rating
0	4,120	0	0	0	0	0	0
1	4,120	0	0	0	0	0	0
2	5,200	1,080	0	1,080	1,080	0	1,080
3	6,360	2,240	0	2,240	1,160	0	1,160
4	6,840	2,720	0	2,720	480	0	480
5	7,200	3,080	0	3,080	360	0	360
6	7,720	3,600	0	3,600	520	0	520
7	8,000	3,880	0	3,880	280	0	280
8	8,080	4,080	120	4,200	200	120	320
9	7,800	4,120	440	4,560	40	320	360
10	7,520	4,240	840	5,080	120	400	520
10.0	7,542	4,262	840	5,102	22	0	22
10.0	Totals	4,262	840	5,102	4,262	840	5,102

Notes

Route:

352 to 390:	Mirror Meadow Trail
390 to 388:	Snow Creek Trail
388 to 306:	Indian Ridge Trail
306 to 308:	North Dome Trail

See 4A for opposite direction

Map Location

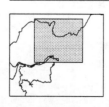

Mirror Lake Trailhead to North Dome

M2   Publisher: O'Neill Software, P.O. Box 26111, San Francisco CA 94126 (415/398-2255)

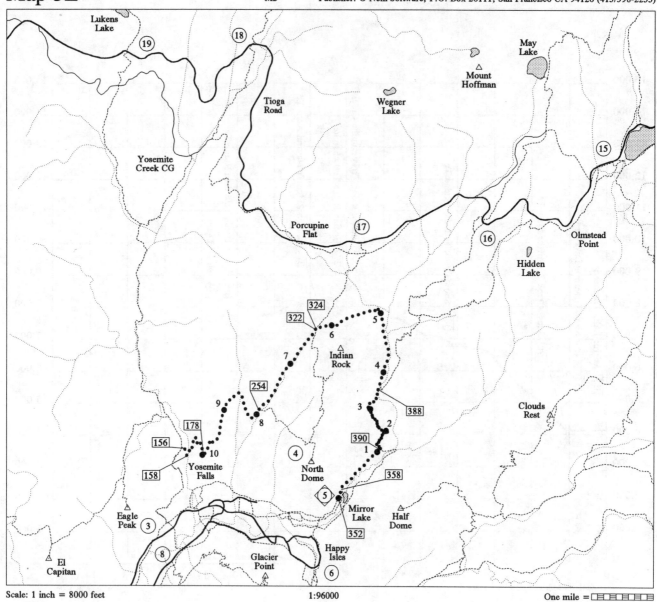

Scale: 1 inch = 8000 feet   1:96000   One mile = ▭▭▭▭▭▭

Destination Chart

Num	Location	Elevation	Cumulative Distances				Incremental Distances			
			Miles	Up	Down	Total	Miles	Up	Down	Total
352	Mirror Lake Trailhead	4,120	0.0	0	0	0	0.0	0	0	0
358	Mirror Mdw Tr/Mirror Lake Tr	4,120	0.2	0	0	0	0.2	0	0	0
390	Snow Creek Tr/Mirror Mdw Tr	4,120	1.1	0	0	0	0.9	0	0	0
388	Snow Creek Tr/Indian Ridge Tr	6,720	3.7	2,600	0	2,600	2.6	2,600	0	2,600
324	Indian Ridge Tr/Porcupine Creek Tr	7,840	6.3	3,720	0	3,720	2.6	1,120	0	1,120
322	Indian Ridge Tr/Lehamite Tr	7,840	6.3	3,720	0	3,720	0.0	0	0	0
254	North Dome Tr/Lehamite Tr	7,000	7.9	3,720	840	4,560	1.6	0	840	840
178	Yosemite Point	7,000	10.0	4,160	1,280	5,440	2.1	440	440	880
156	North Dome Tr/Tr to Yosemite Falls	6,680	10.8	4,240	1,680	5,920	0.8	80	400	480
158	Top of Yosemite Falls	6,680	10.9	4,240	1,680	5,920	0.1	0	0	0
		Totals	10.9	4,240	1,680	5,920	10.9	4,240	1,680	5,920

Mirror Lake Trailhead to Top of Yosemite Falls   5E

Publisher: O'Neill Software, P.O. Box 26111, San Francisco CA 94126 (415/398-2255)

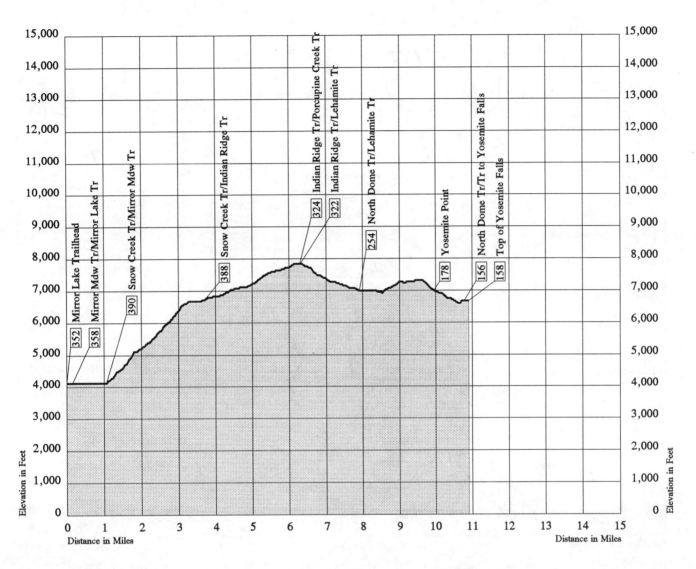

Mileage Chart

Mile	Elevation	Cumulative Distances			Incremental Distances		
		Up	Down	Rating	Up	Down	Rating
0	4,120	0	0	0	0	0	0
1	4,120	0	0	0	0	0	0
2	5,200	1,080	0	1,080	1,080	0	1,080
3	6,360	2,240	0	2,240	1,160	0	1,160
4	6,840	2,720	0	2,720	480	0	480
5	7,200	3,080	0	3,080	360	0	360
6	7,720	3,600	0	3,600	520	0	520
7	7,360	3,720	480	4,200	120	480	600
8	7,000	3,720	840	4,560	0	360	360
9	7,280	4,080	920	5,000	360	80	440
10	6,960	4,160	1,320	5,480	80	400	480
10.9	6,680	4,240	1,680	5,920	80	360	440
10.9	Totals	4,240	1,680	5,920	4,240	1,680	5,920

Notes

Route:

352 to 390:	Mirror Meadow Trail
390 to 388:	Snow Creek Trail
388 to 322:	Indian Ridge Trail
322 to 254:	Lehamite Trail
254 to 156:	North Dome Trail
156 to 158:	Trail to Yosemite Falls

Trail from 322 to 254 not measured

Map Location

Mirror Lake Trailhead to Top of Yosemite Falls

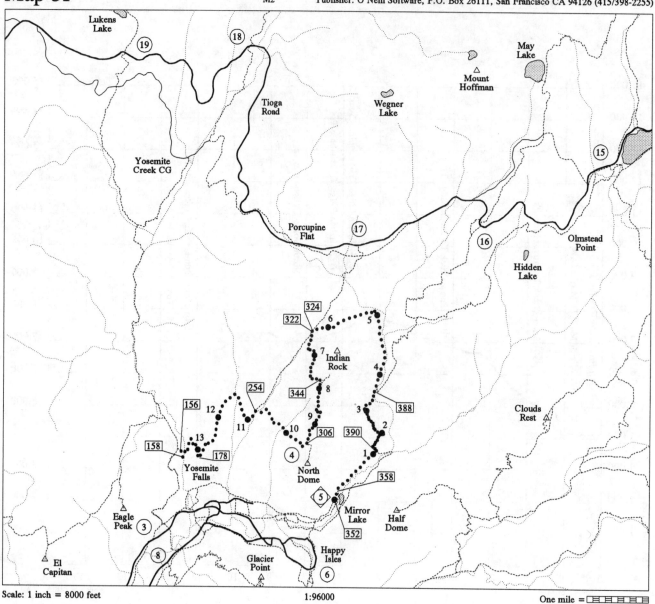

Scale: 1 inch = 8000 feet   1:96000   One mile =

Destination Chart

Num	Location	Elevation	Cumulative Distances				Incremental Distances			
			Miles	Up	Down	Total	Miles	Up	Down	Total
352	Mirror Lake Trailhead	4,120	0.0	0	0	0	0.0	0	0	0
358	Mirror Mdw Tr/Mirror Lake Tr	4,120	0.2	0	0	0	0.2	0	0	0
390	Snow Creek Tr/Mirror Mdw Tr	4,120	1.1	0	0	0	0.9	0	0	0
388	Snow Creek Tr/Indian Ridge Tr	6,720	3.7	2,600	0	2,600	2.6	2,600	0	2,600
324	Indian Ridge Tr/Porcupine Creek Tr	7,840	6.3	3,720	0	3,720	2.6	1,120	0	1,120
322	Indian Ridge Tr/Lehamite Tr	7,840	6.3	3,720	0	3,720	0.0	0	0	0
344	Indian Ridge Tr/Natural Arch Tr	8,120	7.8	4,080	80	4,160	1.5	360	80	440
306	North Dome Tr/Indian Ridge Tr	7,560	9.5	4,120	680	4,800	1.7	40	600	640
254	North Dome Tr/Lehamite Tr	7,000	10.8	4,240	1,360	5,600	1.3	120	680	800
178	Yosemite Point	7,000	12.8	4,680	1,800	6,480	2.0	440	440	880
156	North Dome Tr/Tr to Yosemite Falls	6,680	13.7	4,760	2,200	6,960	0.9	80	400	480
158	Top of Yosemite Falls	6,680	13.8	4,760	2,200	6,960	0.1	0	0	0
		Totals	13.8	4,760	2,200	6,960	13.8	4,760	2,200	6,960

Mirror Lake Trailhead to Top of Yosemite Falls   5F

Publisher: O'Neill Software, P.O. Box 26111, San Francisco CA 94126 (415/398-2255)

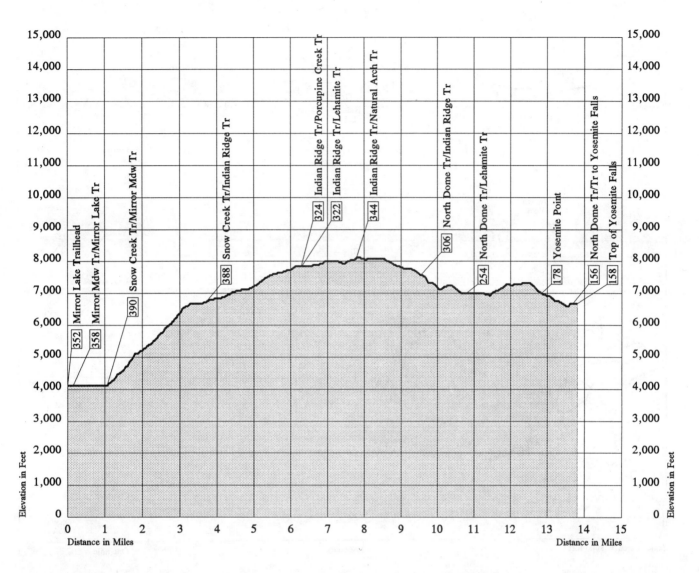

Mileage Chart

		Cumulative Distances			Incremental Distances		
Mile	Elevation	Up	Down	Rating	Up	Down	Rating
0	4,120	0	0	0	0	0	0
1	4,120	0	0	0	0	0	0
2	5,200	1,080	0	1,080	1,080	0	1,080
3	6,360	2,240	0	2,240	1,160	0	1,160
4	6,840	2,720	0	2,720	480	0	480
5	7,200	3,080	0	3,080	360	0	360
6	7,720	3,600	0	3,600	520	0	520
7	8,000	3,880	0	3,880	280	0	280
8	8,080	4,080	120	4,200	200	120	320
9	7,800	4,120	440	4,560	40	320	360
10	7,160	4,120	1,080	5,200	0	640	640
11	7,000	4,240	1,360	5,600	120	280	400
12	7,240	4,600	1,480	6,080	360	120	480
13	6,920	4,680	1,880	6,560	80	400	480
13.8	6,680	4,760	2,200	6,960	80	320	400
13.8	Totals	4,760	2,200	6,960	4,760	2,200	6,960

Notes

Route:
352 to 390:	Mirror Meadow Trail
390 to 388:	Snow Creek Trail
388 to 306:	Indian Ridge Trail
306 to 156:	North Dome Trail
156 to 158:	Trail to Yosemite Falls

Map Location

5F   **Mirror Lake Trailhead to Top of Yosemite Falls**

M3   Publisher: O'Neill Software, P.O. Box 26111, San Francisco CA 94126 (415/398-2255)

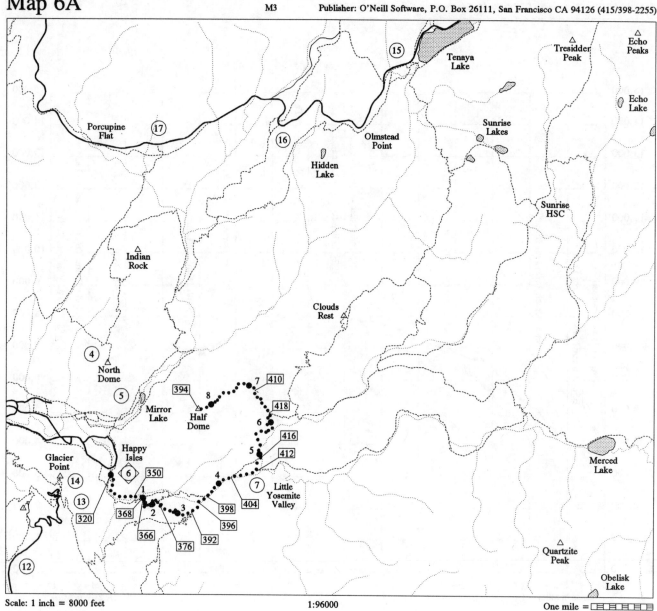

Scale: 1 inch = 8000 feet   1:96000   One mile =

Destination Chart

Num	Location	Elevation	Cumulative Distances				Incremental Distances			
			Miles	Up	Down	Total	Miles	Up	Down	Total
320	Happy Isles Trailhead	4,040	0.0	0	0	0	0.0	0	0	0
350	Vernal Fall Footbridge	4,400	0.8	360	0	360	0.8	360	0	360
368	John Muir Tr/Mist Tr	4,600	0.9	560	0	560	0.1	200	0	200
366	John Muir Tr/Horse Tr	4,600	1.0	560	0	560	0.1	0	0	0
376	John Muir Tr/Crossover Tr	5,480	2.3	1,480	40	1,520	1.3	920	40	960
392	John Muir Tr/Panorama Tr	6,000	3.3	2,040	80	2,120	1.0	560	40	600
396	Nevada Fall Footbridge	5,960	3.5	2,040	120	2,160	0.2	0	40	40
398	John Muir Tr/Mist Tr	5,960	3.7	2,040	120	2,160	0.2	0	0	0
404	John Muir Tr/LYV Bypass	6,120	4.2	2,240	160	2,400	0.5	200	40	240
412	Little Yosemite Valley	6,120	4.7	2,240	160	2,400	0.5	0	0	0
416	John Muir Tr/LYV Bypass	6,120	4.9	2,240	160	2,400	0.2	0	0	0
418	Half Dome Tr/John Muir Tr	7,000	6.2	3,120	160	3,280	1.3	880	0	880
410	Tr to Spring	7,400	6.8	3,520	160	3,680	0.6	400	0	400
394	Half Dome	8,836	8.2	4,996	200	5,196	1.4	1,476	40	1,516
	Totals		8.2	4,996	200	5,196	8.2	4,996	200	5,196

Happy Isles Trailhead to Half Dome   6A

Publisher: O'Neill Software, P.O. Box 26111, San Francisco CA 94126 (415/398-2255)

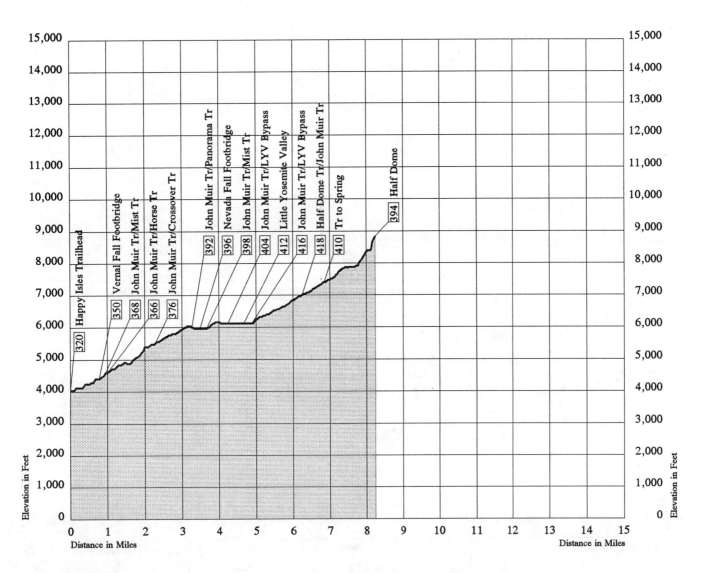

Mileage Chart

Mile	Elevation	Cumulative Distances			Incremental Distances		
		Up	Down	Rating	Up	Down	Rating
0	4,040	0	0	0	0	0	0
1	4,600	560	0	560	560	0	560
2	5,400	1,400	40	1,440	840	40	880
3	5,920	1,920	40	1,960	520	0	520
4	6,160	2,240	120	2,360	320	80	400
5	6,240	2,360	160	2,520	120	40	160
6	6,840	2,960	160	3,120	600	0	600
7	7,480	3,600	160	3,760	640	0	640
8	8,360	4,520	200	4,720	920	40	960
8.2	8,836	4,996	200	5,196	476	0	476
8.2	Totals	4,996	200	5,196	4,996	200	5,196

Notes

Route:
- 320 to 418: John Muir Trail
- 418 to 394: Half Dome Trail

Map Location

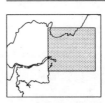

Happy Isles Trailhead to Half Dome

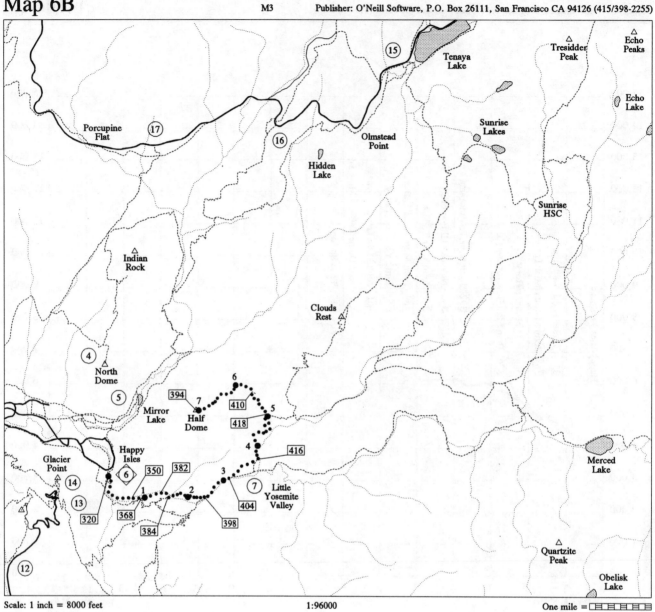

Scale: 1 inch = 8000 feet   1:96000   One mile =

Destination Chart

Num	Location	Elevation	Cumulative Distances				Incremental Distances			
			Miles	Up	Down	Total	Miles	Up	Down	Total
320	Happy Isles Trailhead	4,040	0.0	0	0	0	0.0	0	0	0
350	Vernal Fall Footbridge	4,400	0.8	360	0	360	0.8	360	0	360
368	John Muir Tr/Mist Tr	4,600	0.9	560	0	560	0.1	200	0	200
382	Vernal Fall	5,040	1.3	1,000	0	1,000	0.4	440	0	440
384	Crossover Tr/Mist Tr	5,200	1.5	1,160	0	1,160	0.2	160	0	160
398	John Muir Tr/Mist Tr	5,960	2.5	1,960	40	2,000	1.0	800	40	840
404	John Muir Tr/LYV Bypass	6,120	3.1	2,160	80	2,240	0.6	200	40	240
416	John Muir Tr/LYV Bypass	6,120	3.7	2,200	120	2,320	0.6	40	40	80
418	Half Dome Tr/John Muir Tr	7,000	5.0	3,080	120	3,200	1.3	880	0	880
410	Tr to Spring	7,400	5.6	3,480	120	3,600	0.6	400	0	400
394	Half Dome	8,836	7.0	4,956	160	5,116	1.4	1,476	40	1,516
		Totals	7.0	4,956	160	5,116	7.0	4,956	160	5,116

Happy Isles Trailhead to Half Dome   6B

Publisher: O'Neill Software, P.O. Box 26111, San Francisco CA 94126 (415/398-2255)

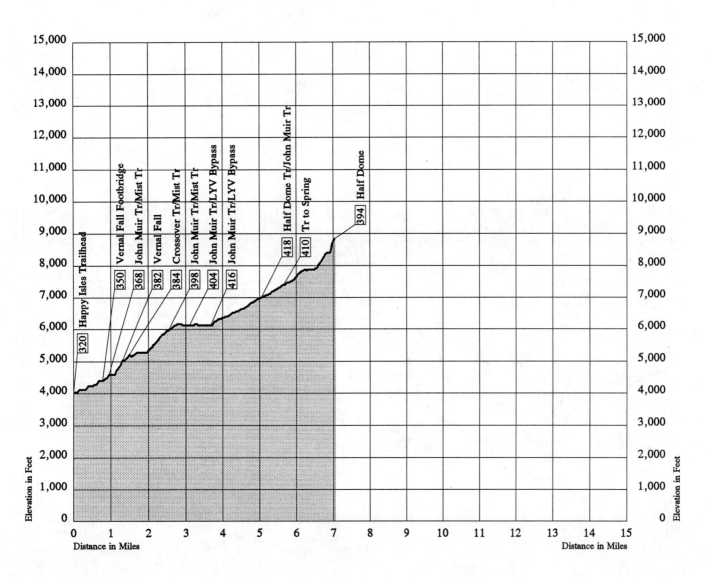

Mileage Chart

		Cumulative Distances			Incremental Distances		
Mile	Elevation	Up	Down	Rating	Up	Down	Rating
0	4,040	0	0	0	0	0	0
1	4,600	560	0	560	560	0	560
2	5,360	1,360	40	1,400	800	40	840
3	6,120	2,160	80	2,240	800	40	840
4	6,360	2,440	120	2,560	280	40	320
5	6,960	3,040	120	3,160	600	0	600
6	7,680	3,760	120	3,880	720	0	720
7	8,760	4,880	160	5,040	1,120	40	1,160
7.0	8,836	4,956	160	5,116	76	0	76
7.0	Totals	4,956	160	5,116	4,956	160	5,116

Notes

Route:

320 to 368:	John Muir Trail
368 to 398:	Mist Trail
398 to 404:	John Muir Trail
404 to 416:	LYV Bypass
416 to 418:	John Muir Trail
418 to 394:	Half Dome Trail

Map Location

Happy Isles Trailhead to Half Dome

Map 6C

M3   Publisher: O'Neill Software, P.O. Box 26111, San Francisco CA 94126 (415/398-2255)

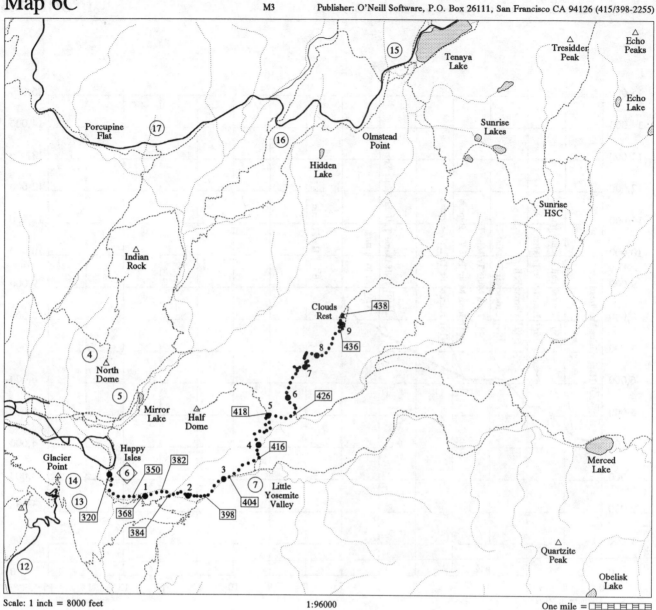

Scale: 1 inch = 8000 feet   1:96000   One mile = ▭▭▭▭▭▭

Destination Chart

Num	Location	Elevation	Cumulative Distances				Incremental Distances			
			Miles	Up	Down	Total	Miles	Up	Down	Total
320	Happy Isles Trailhead	4,040	0.0	0	0	0	0.0	0	0	0
350	Vernal Fall Footbridge	4,400	0.8	360	0	360	0.8	360	0	360
368	John Muir Tr/Mist Tr	4,600	0.9	560	0	560	0.1	200	0	200
382	Vernal Fall	5,040	1.3	1,000	0	1,000	0.4	440	0	440
384	Crossover Tr/Mist Tr	5,200	1.5	1,160	0	1,160	0.2	160	0	160
398	John Muir Tr/Mist Tr	5,960	2.5	1,960	40	2,000	1.0	800	40	840
404	John Muir Tr/LYV Bypass	6,120	3.1	2,160	80	2,240	0.6	200	40	240
416	John Muir Tr/LYV Bypass	6,120	3.7	2,200	120	2,320	0.6	40	40	80
418	Half Dome Tr/John Muir Tr	7,000	5.0	3,080	120	3,200	1.3	880	0	880
426	Clouds Rest Tr/John Muir Tr	7,200	5.5	3,280	120	3,400	0.5	200	0	200
436	Clouds Rest Bypass/Clouds Rest Tr	9,360	8.7	5,440	120	5,560	3.2	2,160	0	2,160
438	Clouds Rest	9,926	9.4	6,006	120	6,126	0.7	566	0	566
	Totals		9.4	6,006	120	6,126	9.4	6,006	120	6,126

Happy Isles Trailhead to Clouds Rest

6C

Publisher: O'Neill Software, P.O. Box 26111, San Francisco CA 94126 (415/398-2255)

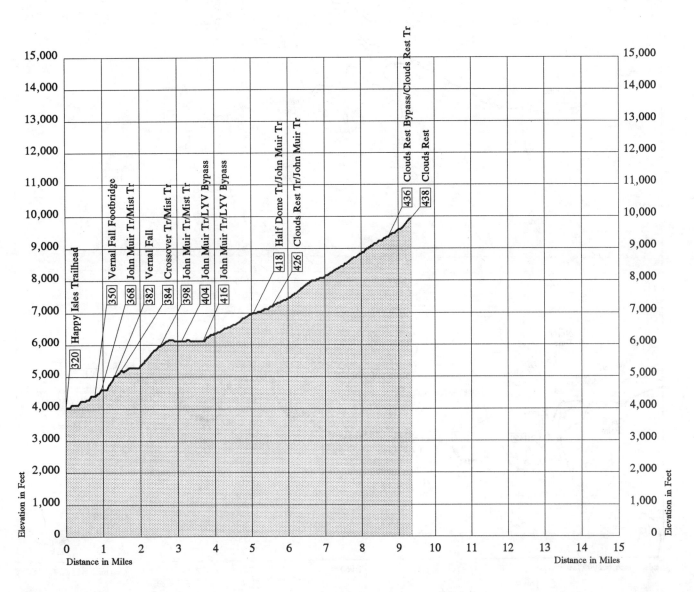

Mileage Chart

Mile	Elevation	Cumulative Distances			Incremental Distances		
		Up	Down	Rating	Up	Down	Rating
0	4,040	0	0	0	0	0	0
1	4,600	560	0	560	560	0	560
2	5,360	1,360	40	1,400	800	40	840
3	6,120	2,160	80	2,240	800	40	840
4	6,360	2,440	120	2,560	280	40	320
5	6,960	3,040	120	3,160	600	0	600
6	7,440	3,520	120	3,640	480	0	480
7	8,120	4,200	120	4,320	680	0	680
8	8,840	4,920	120	5,040	720	0	720
9	9,600	5,680	120	5,800	760	0	760
9.4	9,926	6,006	120	6,126	326	0	326
9.4	Totals	6,006	120	6,126	6,006	120	6,126

Notes

Route:
320 to 368:	John Muir Trail
368 to 398:	Mist Trail
398 to 404:	John Muir Trail
404 to 416:	LYV Bypass
416 to 426:	John Muir Trail
426 to 438:	Clouds Rest Trail

Map Location

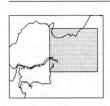

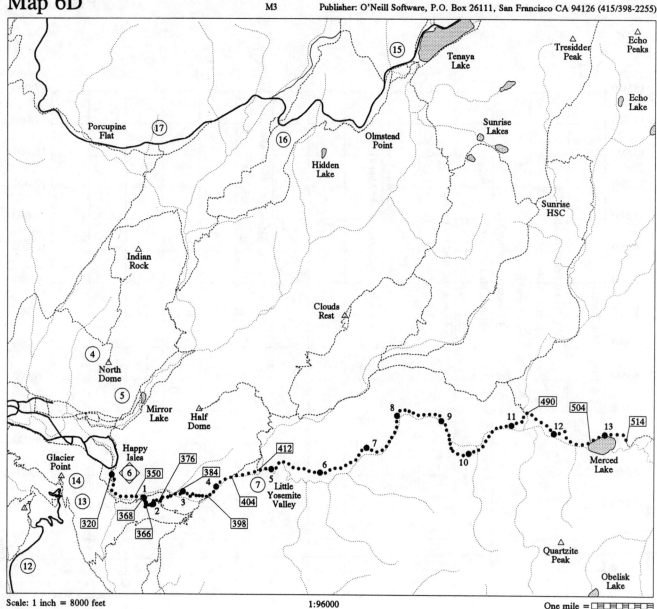

Scale: 1 inch = 8000 feet   1:96000   One mile = □□□□□□

Destination Chart

Num	Location	Elevation	Cumulative Distances				Incremental Distances			
			Miles	Up	Down	Total	Miles	Up	Down	Total
320	Happy Isles Trailhead	4,040	0.0	0	0	0	0.0	0	0	0
350	Vernal Fall Footbridge	4,400	0.8	360	0	360	0.8	360	0	360
368	John Muir Tr/Mist Tr	4,600	0.9	560	0	560	0.1	200	0	200
366	John Muir Tr/Horse Tr	4,600	1.0	560	0	560	0.1	0	0	0
376	John Muir Tr/Crossover Tr	5,480	2.3	1,480	40	1,520	1.3	920	40	960
384	Crossover Tr/Mist Tr	5,200	2.7	1,480	320	1,800	0.4	0	280	280
398	John Muir Tr/Mist Tr	5,960	3.8	2,280	360	2,640	1.1	800	40	840
404	John Muir Tr/LYV Bypass	6,120	4.3	2,480	400	2,880	0.5	200	40	240
412	Little Yosemite Valley	6,120	4.8	2,480	400	2,880	0.5	0	0	0
490	Echo Valley	7,000	11.4	3,520	560	4,080	6.6	1,040	160	1,200
504	Merced Lake	7,200	12.7	3,720	560	4,280	1.3	200	0	200
514	Merced Lake HSC	7,200	13.4	3,720	560	4,280	0.7	0	0	0
		Totals	13.4	3,720	560	4,280	13.4	3,720	560	4,280

Happy Isles Trailhead to Merced Lake HSC

Publisher: O'Neill Software, P.O. Box 26111, San Francisco CA 94126 (415/398-2255)

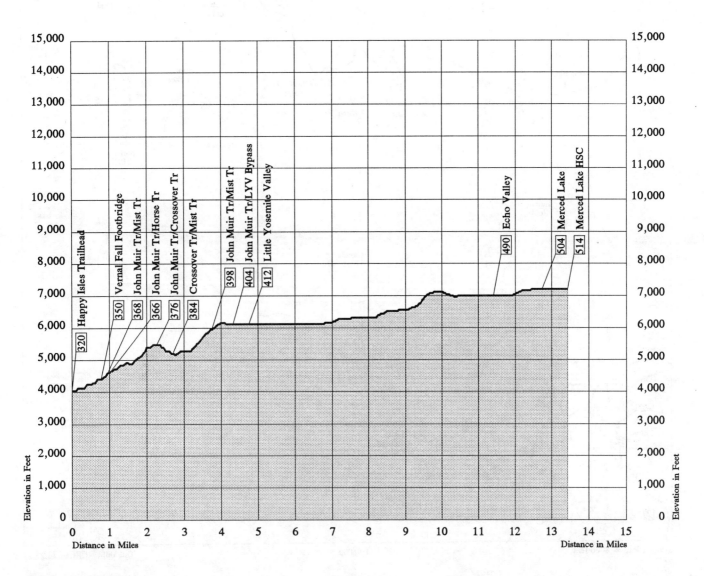

Mileage Chart

		Cumulative Distances			Incremental Distances		
Mile	Elevation	Up	Down	Rating	Up	Down	Rating
0	4,040	0	0	0	0	0	0
1	4,600	560	0	560	560	0	560
2	5,400	1,400	40	1,440	840	40	880
3	5,280	1,600	360	1,960	200	320	520
4	6,160	2,480	360	2,840	880	0	880
5	6,120	2,480	400	2,880	0	40	40
6	6,120	2,480	400	2,880	0	0	0
7	6,160	2,520	400	2,920	40	0	40
8	6,320	2,680	400	3,080	160	0	160
9	6,560	2,920	400	3,320	240	0	240
10	7,120	3,480	400	3,880	560	0	560
11	7,000	3,520	560	4,080	40	160	200
12	7,040	3,560	560	4,120	40	0	40
13	7,200	3,720	560	4,280	160	0	160
13.4	7,200	3,720	560	4,280	0	0	0
13.4	Totals	3,720	560	4,280	3,720	560	4,280

Notes

Route:

320 to 376:	John Muir Trail
376 to 384:	Crossover Trail
384 to 398:	Mist Trail
398 to 412:	John Muir Trail
412 to 514:	Merced Lake Trail

Map Location

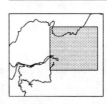

Happy Isles Trailhead to Merced Lake HSC

M3   Publisher: O'Neill Software, P.O. Box 26111, San Francisco CA 94126 (415/398-2255)

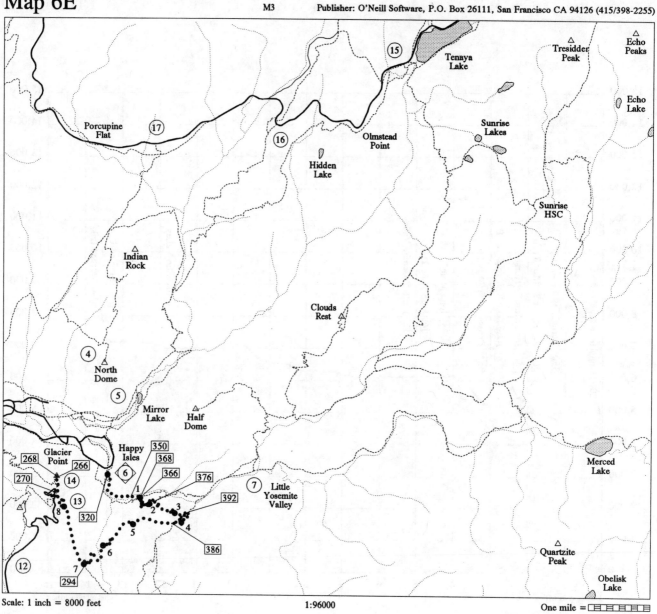

Scale: 1 inch = 8000 feet   1:96000   One mile =

Destination Chart

Num	Location	Elevation	Cumulative Distances				Incremental Distances			
			Miles	Up	Down	Total	Miles	Up	Down	Total
320	Happy Isles Trailhead	4,040	0.0	0	0	0	0.0	0	0	0
350	Vernal Fall Footbridge	4,400	0.8	360	0	360	0.8	360	0	360
368	John Muir Tr/Mist Tr	4,600	0.9	560	0	560	0.1	200	0	200
366	John Muir Tr/Horse Tr	4,600	1.0	560	0	560	0.1	0	0	0
376	John Muir Tr/Crossover Tr	5,480	2.3	1,480	40	1,520	1.3	920	40	960
392	John Muir Tr/Panorama Tr	6,000	3.3	2,040	80	2,120	1.0	560	40	600
386	Panorama Tr/Mono Meadow Tr	6,600	4.3	2,640	80	2,720	1.0	600	0	600
294	Panorama Tr/Buena Vista Tr	6,440	7.0	3,200	800	4,000	2.7	560	720	1,280
270	Panorama Trailhead	7,280	8.6	4,040	800	4,840	1.6	840	0	840
266	Glacier Point Tr	7,200	8.8	4,080	920	5,000	0.2	40	120	160
268	Glacier Point	7,214	8.9	4,094	920	5,014	0.1	14	0	14
	Totals		8.9	4,094	920	5,014	8.9	4,094	920	5,014

Happy Isles Trailhead to Glacier Point

Publisher: O'Neill Software, P.O. Box 26111, San Francisco CA 94126 (415/398-2255)

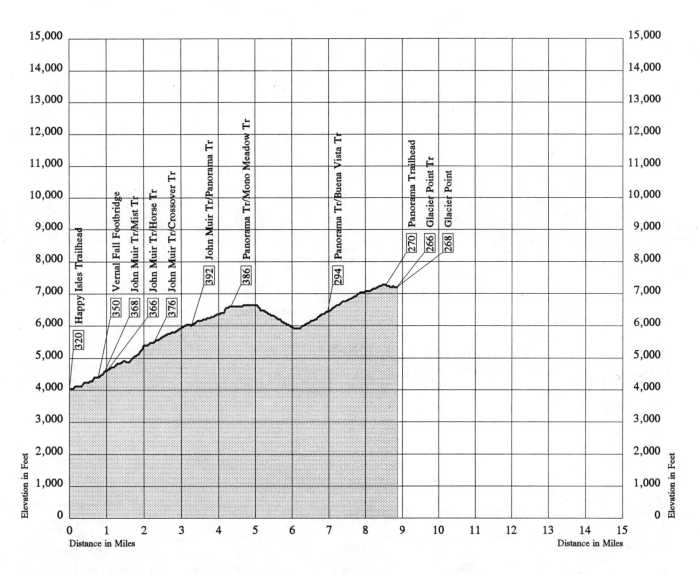

Mileage Chart

Mile	Elevation	Cumulative Distances			Incremental Distances		
		Up	Down	Rating	Up	Down	Rating
0	4,040	0	0	0	0	0	0
1	4,600	560	0	560	560	0	560
2	5,400	1,400	40	1,440	840	40	880
3	5,920	1,920	40	1,960	520	0	520
4	6,360	2,400	80	2,480	480	40	520
5	6,640	2,680	80	2,760	280	0	280
6	5,960	2,680	760	3,440	0	680	680
7	6,440	3,200	800	4,000	520	40	560
8	7,080	3,840	800	4,640	640	0	640
8.9	7,214	4,094	920	5,014	254	120	374
8.9	Totals	4,094	920	5,014	4,094	920	5,014

Notes

Route:
320 to 392:   John Muir Trail
392 to 270:   Panorama Trail
270 to 268:   Glacier Point Trail

See 13A for opposite direction (to 270)

Map Location

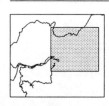

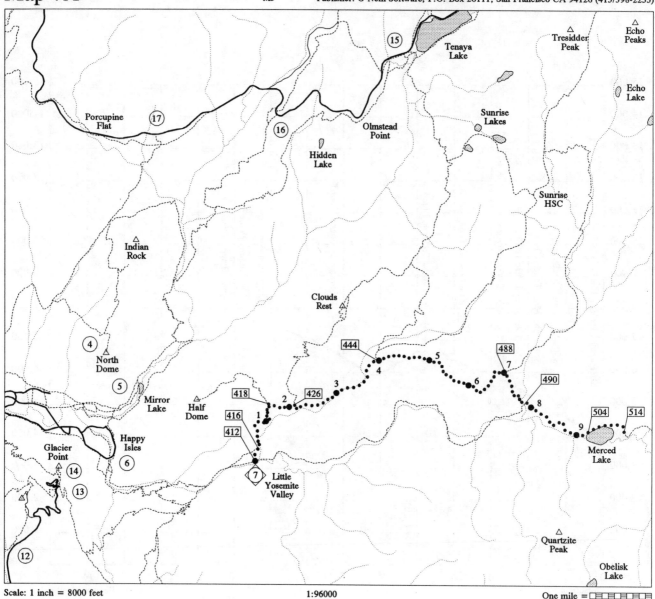

Scale: 1 inch = 8000 feet   1:96000   One mile =

Destination Chart

Num	Location	Elevation	Cumulative Distances				Incremental Distances			
			Miles	Up	Down	Total	Miles	Up	Down	Total
412	Little Yosemite Valley	6,120	0.0	0	0	0	0.0	0	0	0
416	John Muir Tr/LYV Bypass	6,120	0.2	0	0	0	0.2	0	0	0
418	Half Dome Tr/John Muir Tr	7,000	1.6	880	0	880	1.4	880	0	880
426	Clouds Rest Tr/John Muir Tr	7,200	2.1	1,080	0	1,080	0.5	200	0	200
444	John Muir Tr/High Tr	7,880	4.0	1,800	40	1,840	1.9	720	40	760
488	Echo Creek Tr/High Tr	7,480	7.0	1,880	520	2,400	3.0	80	480	560
490	Echo Valley	7,000	7.9	1,880	1,000	2,880	0.9	0	480	480
504	Merced Lake	7,200	9.2	2,080	1,000	3,080	1.3	200	0	200
514	Merced Lake HSC	7,200	9.9	2,080	1,000	3,080	0.7	0	0	0
	Totals		9.9	2,080	1,000	3,080	9.9	2,080	1,000	3,080

Little Yosemite Valley to Merced Lake HSC

7A

Publisher: O'Neill Software, P.O. Box 26111, San Francisco CA 94126 (415/398-2255)

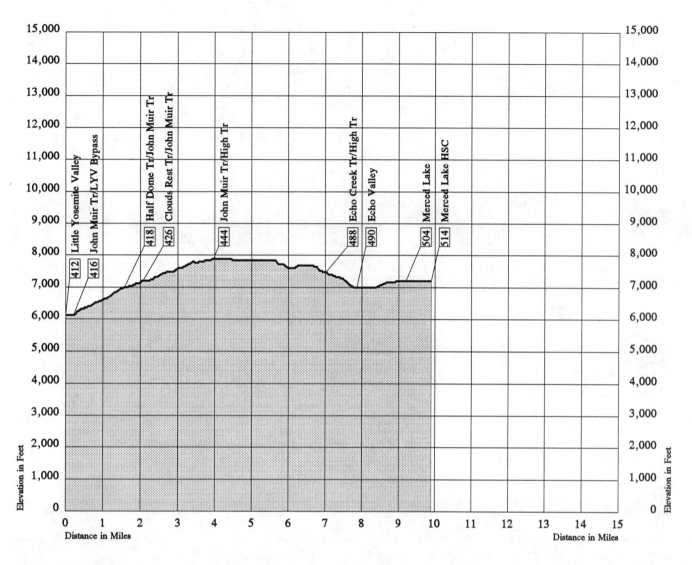

Mileage Chart

		Cumulative Distances			Incremental Distances		
Mile	Elevation	Up	Down	Rating	Up	Down	Rating
0	6,120	0	0	0	0	0	0
1	6,600	480	0	480	480	0	480
2	7,160	1,040	0	1,040	560	0	560
3	7,560	1,440	0	1,440	400	0	400
4	7,880	1,800	40	1,840	360	40	400
5	7,840	1,800	80	1,880	0	40	40
6	7,600	1,800	320	2,120	0	240	240
7	7,480	1,880	520	2,400	80	200	280
8	7,000	1,880	1,000	2,880	0	480	480
9	7,200	2,080	1,000	3,080	200	0	200
9.9	7,200	2,080	1,000	3,080	0	0	0
9.9	Totals	2,080	1,000	3,080	2,080	1,000	3,080

Notes

Route:

412 to 444:	John Muir Trail
444 to 490:	High Trail
490 to 514:	Merced Lake Trail

Map Location

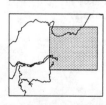

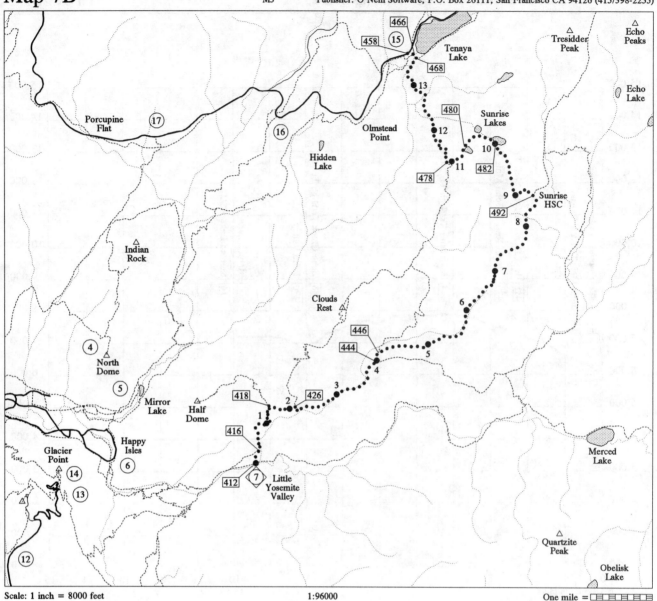

Scale: 1 inch = 8000 feet   1:96000   One mile =

Destination Chart

Num	Location	Elevation	Cumulative Distances				Incremental Distances			
			Miles	Up	Down	Total	Miles	Up	Down	Total
412	Little Yosemite Valley	6,120	0.0	0	0	0	0.0	0	0	0
416	John Muir Tr/LYV Bypass	6,120	0.2	0	0	0	0.2	0	0	0
418	Half Dome Tr/John Muir Tr	7,000	1.6	880	0	880	1.4	880	0	880
426	Clouds Rest Tr/John Muir Tr	7,200	2.1	1,080	0	1,080	0.5	200	0	200
444	John Muir Tr/High Tr	7,880	4.0	1,800	40	1,840	1.9	720	40	760
446	John Muir Tr/Sunrise Creek Tr	8,000	4.1	1,920	40	1,960	0.1	120	0	120
492	Sunrise Lake Tr/John Muir Tr	9,320	8.6	3,600	400	4,000	4.5	1,680	360	2,040
482	Sunrise Lake	9,440	10.0	4,040	720	4,760	1.4	440	320	760
480	Sunrise Lake	9,200	10.6	4,040	960	5,000	0.6	0	240	240
478	Forsyth Tr/Sunrise Lakes Tr	9,200	11.1	4,080	1,000	5,080	0.5	40	40	80
468	Forsyth Tr/Tenaya Lake Tr	8,160	13.6	4,080	2,040	6,120	2.5	0	1,040	1,040
466	Tenaya Lake CG	8,160	13.7	4,080	2,040	6,120	0.1	0	0	0
458	Tenaya Lake Trailhead	8,200	13.8	4,120	2,040	6,160	0.1	40	0	40
	Totals		13.8	4,120	2,040	6,160	13.8	4,120	2,040	6,160

Little Yosemite Valley to Tenaya Lake Trailhead   7B

Publisher: O'Neill Software, P.O. Box 26111, San Francisco CA 94126 (415/398-2255)

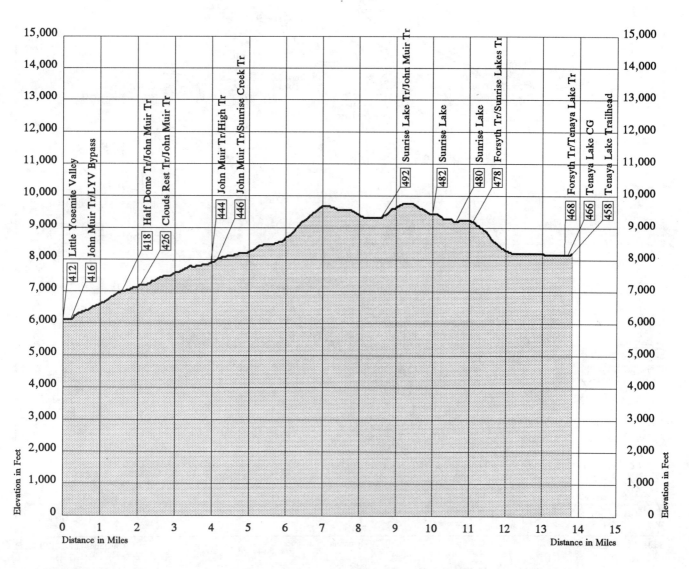

Mileage Chart

Mile	Elevation	Cumulative Distances			Incremental Distances		
		Up	Down	Rating	Up	Down	Rating
0	6,120	0	0	0	0	0	0
1	6,600	480	0	480	480	0	480
2	7,160	1,040	0	1,040	560	0	560
3	7,560	1,440	0	1,440	400	0	400
4	7,920	1,840	40	1,880	400	40	440
5	8,240	2,160	40	2,200	320	0	320
6	8,720	2,640	40	2,680	480	0	480
7	9,680	3,600	40	3,640	960	0	960
8	9,400	3,600	320	3,920	0	280	280
9	9,640	3,920	400	4,320	320	80	400
10	9,440	4,040	720	4,760	120	320	440
11	9,240	4,080	960	5,040	40	240	280
12	8,280	4,080	1,920	6,000	0	960	960
13	8,200	4,080	2,000	6,080	0	80	80
13.8	8,200	4,120	2,040	6,160	40	40	80
13.8	Totals	4,120	2,040	6,160	4,120	2,040	6,160

Notes

Route:
412 to 492:	John Muir Trail
492 to 478:	Sunrise Lakes Trail
478 to 468:	Forsyth Trail
468 to 458:	Tenaya Lake Trail

See 15B for opposite direction

Map Location

Little Yosemite Valley to Tenaya Lake Trailhead

M3   Publisher: O'Neill Software, P.O. Box 26111, San Francisco CA 94126 (415/398-2255)

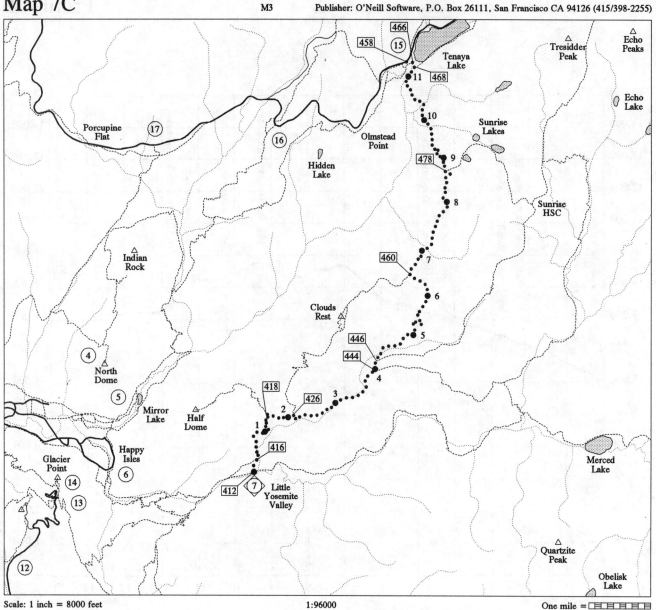

Scale: 1 inch = 8000 feet   1:96000   One mile = ▭▭▭▭▭▭

Destination Chart

Num	Location	Elevation	Cumulative Distances				Incremental Distances			
			Miles	Up	Down	Total	Miles	Up	Down	Total
412	Little Yosemite Valley	6,120	0.0	0	0	0	0.0	0	0	0
416	John Muir Tr/LYV Bypass	6,120	0.2	0	0	0	0.2	0	0	0
418	Half Dome Tr/John Muir Tr	7,000	1.6	880	0	880	1.4	880	0	880
426	Clouds Rest Tr/John Muir Tr	7,200	2.1	1,080	0	1,080	0.5	200	0	200
444	John Muir Tr/High Tr	7,880	4.0	1,800	40	1,840	1.9	720	40	760
446	John Muir Tr/Sunrise Creek Tr	8,000	4.1	1,920	40	1,960	0.1	120	0	120
460	Forsyth Tr/Clouds Rest Tr	9,120	6.5	3,040	40	3,080	2.4	1,120	0	1,120
478	Forsyth Tr/Sunrise Lakes Tr	9,200	8.7	3,440	360	3,800	2.2	400	320	720
468	Forsyth Tr/Tenaya Lake Tr	8,160	11.2	3,440	1,400	4,840	2.5	0	1,040	1,040
466	Tenaya Lake CG	8,160	11.3	3,440	1,400	4,840	0.1	0	0	0
458	Tenaya Lake Trailhead	8,200	11.4	3,480	1,400	4,880	0.1	40	0	40
		Totals	11.4	3,480	1,400	4,880	11.4	3,480	1,400	4,880

Little Yosemite Valley to Tenaya Lake Trailhead

Publisher: O'Neill Software, P.O. Box 26111, San Francisco CA 94126 (415/398-2255)

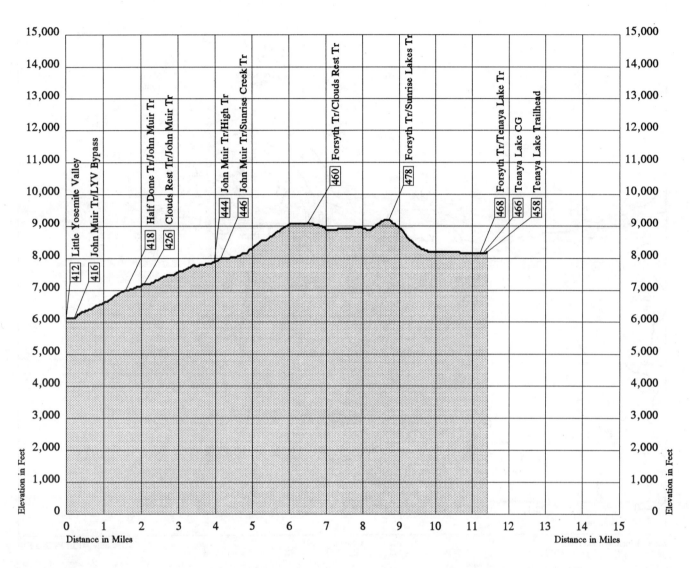

Mileage Chart

		Cumulative Distances			Incremental Distances		
Mile	Elevation	Up	Down	Rating	Up	Down	Rating
0	6,120	0	0	0	0	0	0
1	6,600	480	0	480	480	0	480
2	7,160	1,040	0	1,040	560	0	560
3	7,560	1,440	0	1,440	400	0	400
4	7,920	1,840	40	1,880	400	40	440
5	8,320	2,240	40	2,280	400	0	400
6	9,080	3,000	40	3,040	760	0	760
7	8,880	3,040	280	3,320	40	240	280
8	8,920	3,120	320	3,440	80	40	120
9	8,920	3,440	640	4,080	320	320	640
10	8,200	3,440	1,360	4,800	0	720	720
11	8,160	3,440	1,400	4,840	0	40	40
11.4	8,200	3,480	1,400	4,880	40	0	40
11.4	Totals	3,480	1,400	4,880	3,480	1,400	4,880

Notes

Route:
  412 to 446:   John Muir Trail
  446 to 468:   Forsyth Trail
  468 to 458:   Tenaya Lake Trail

See 15C for opposite direction

Map Location

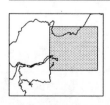

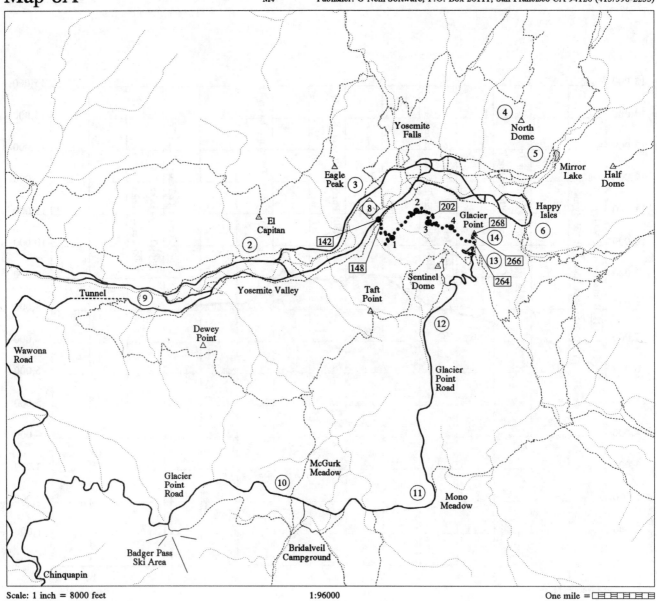

Scale: 1 inch = 8000 feet   1:96000   One mile =

Destination Chart

Num	Location	Elevation	Cumulative Distances				Incremental Distances			
			Miles	Up	Down	Total	Miles	Up	Down	Total
142	Four Mile Trailhead	4,000	0.0	0	0	0	0.0	0	0	0
148	Four Mile Tr/Valley Tr	4,000	0.1	0	0	0	0.1	0	0	0
202	Union Point	6,360	2.9	2,360	0	2,360	2.8	2,360	0	2,360
264	Four Mile Tr/Glacier Point Tr	7,160	4.6	3,160	0	3,160	1.7	800	0	800
266	Glacier Point Tr	7,200	4.8	3,200	0	3,200	0.2	40	0	40
268	Glacier Point	7,214	4.8	3,214	0	3,214	0.0	14	0	14
	Totals		4.8	3,214	0	3,214	4.8	3,214	0	3,214

Publisher: O'Neill Software, P.O. Box 26111, San Francisco CA 94126 (415/398-2255)

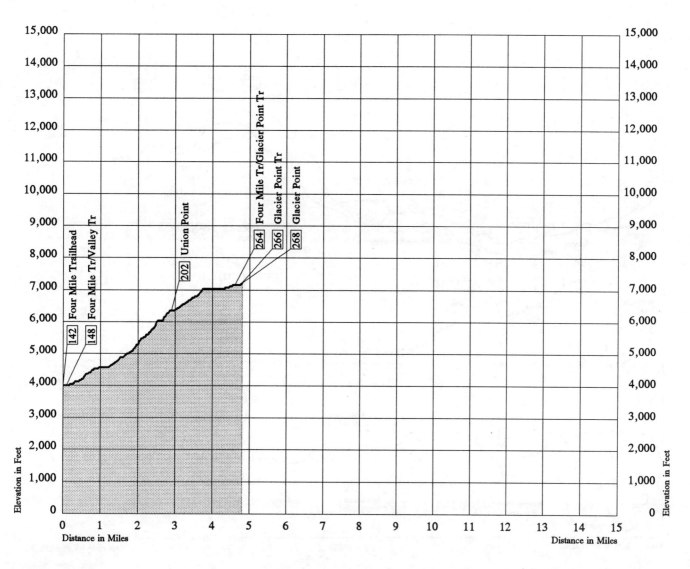

Mileage Chart

Mile	Elevation	Cumulative Distances			Incremental Distances		
		Up	Down	Rating	Up	Down	Rating
0	4,000	0	0	0	0	0	0
1	4,560	560	0	560	560	0	560
2	5,280	1,280	0	1,280	720	0	720
3	6,400	2,400	0	2,400	1,120	0	1,120
4	7,040	3,040	0	3,040	640	0	640
4.8	7,214	3,214	0	3,214	174	0	174
4.8	Totals	3,214	0	3,214	3,214	0	3,214

Notes

Route:

   142 to 264:   Four Mile Trail
   264 to 268:   Glacier Point Trail

See 14A for opposite direction

Map Location

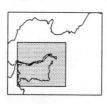

Four Mile Trailhead to Glacier Point

M4   Publisher: O'Neill Software, P.O. Box 26111, San Francisco CA 94126 (415/398-2255)

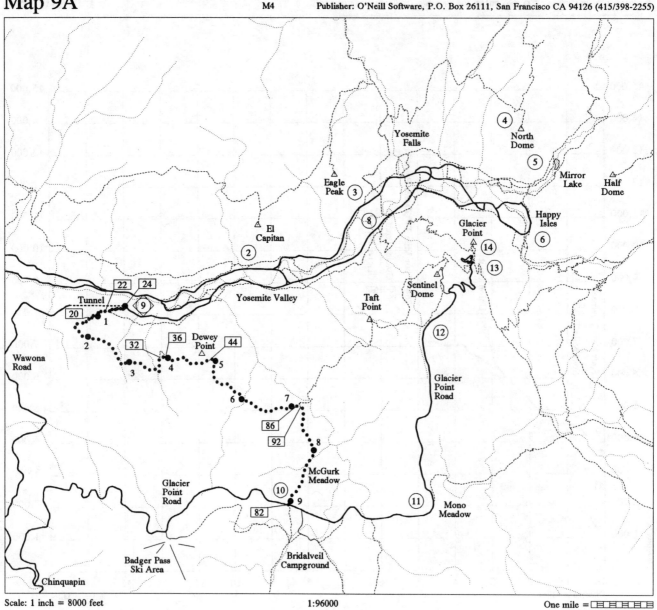

Scale: 1 inch = 8000 feet   1:96000   One mile =

Destination Chart

Num	Location	Elevation	Cumulative Distances				Incremental Distances			
			Miles	Up	Down	Total	Miles	Up	Down	Total
24	Discovery View Overlook	4,400	0.0	0	0	0	0.0	0	0	0
22	Pohono Tr/Old Wawona Rd	4,920	0.7	520	0	520	0.7	520	0	520
20	Inspiration Point	5,440	1.3	1,040	0	1,040	0.6	520	0	520
32	Pohono Tr/Stanford Point Tr	6,800	3.8	2,560	160	2,720	2.5	1,520	160	1,680
36	Pohono Tr/Stanford Point Tr	6,760	3.9	2,560	200	2,760	0.1	0	40	40
44	Pohono Tr/Dewey Point Rt	7,360	4.8	3,160	200	3,360	0.9	600	0	600
86	Pohono Tr/McGurk Meadow Tr	6,800	7.1	3,200	800	4,000	2.3	40	600	640
92	Pohono Tr/McGurk Meadow Tr	6,800	7.2	3,200	800	4,000	0.1	0	0	0
82	McGurk Meadow Trailhead	7,080	9.1	3,520	840	4,360	1.9	320	40	360
	Totals		9.1	3,520	840	4,360	9.1	3,520	840	4,360

Discovery View Overlook to McGurk Meadow Trailhead   9A

Publisher: O'Neill Software, P.O. Box 26111, San Francisco CA 94126 (415/398-2255)

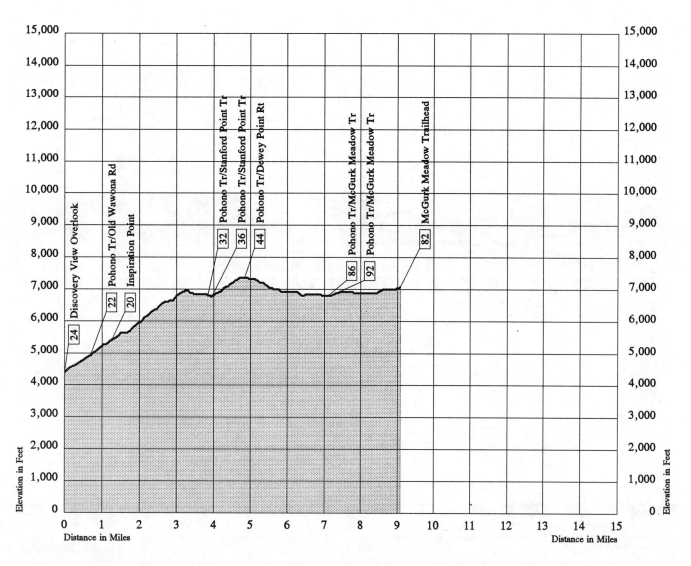

Mileage Chart

Mile	Elevation	Cumulative Distances			Incremental Distances		
		Up	Down	Rating	Up	Down	Rating
0	4,400	0	0	0	0	0	0
1	5,240	840	0	840	840	0	840
2	5,960	1,560	0	1,560	720	0	720
3	6,800	2,400	0	2,400	840	0	840
4	6,800	2,600	200	2,800	200	200	400
5	7,320	3,160	240	3,400	560	40	600
6	6,920	3,160	640	3,800	0	400	400
7	6,800	3,200	800	4,000	40	160	200
8	6,880	3,320	840	4,160	120	40	160
9	7,040	3,480	840	4,320	160	0	160
9.1	7,080	3,520	840	4,360	40	0	40
9.1	Totals	3,520	840	4,360	3,520	840	4,360

Notes

Route:
- 24 to 86: Pohono Trail
- 86 to 82: McGurk Meadow Trail

See 10A for opposite direction

Map Location

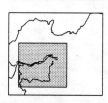

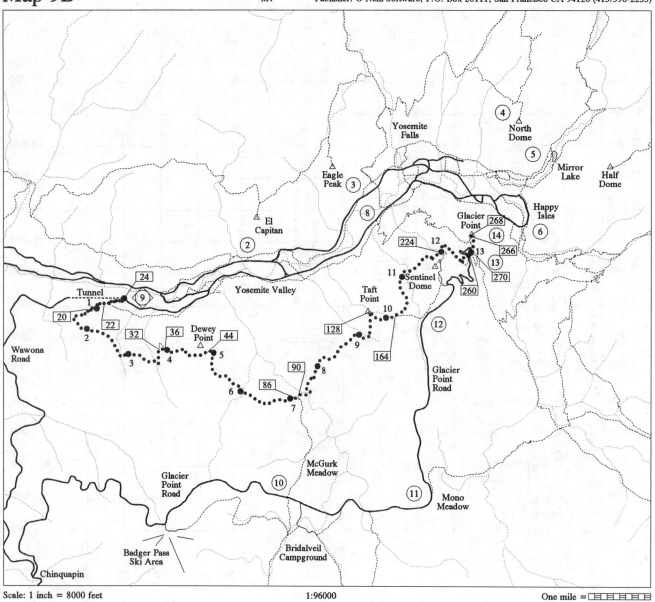

Scale: 1 inch = 8000 feet   1:96000   One mile =

Destination Chart

Num	Location	Elevation	Cumulative Distances				Incremental Distances			
			Miles	Up	Down	Total	Miles	Up	Down	Total
24	Discovery View Overlook	4,400	0.0	0	0	0	0.0	0	0	0
22	Pohono Tr/Old Wawona Rd	4,920	0.7	520	0	520	0.7	520	0	520
20	Inspiration Point	5,440	1.3	1,040	0	1,040	0.6	520	0	520
32	Pohono Tr/Stanford Point Tr	6,800	3.8	2,560	160	2,720	2.5	1,520	160	1,680
36	Pohono Tr/Stanford Point Tr	6,760	3.9	2,560	200	2,760	0.1	0	40	40
44	Pohono Tr/Dewey Point Rt	7,360	4.8	3,160	200	3,360	0.9	600	0	600
86	Pohono Tr/McGurk Meadow Tr	6,800	7.1	3,200	800	4,000	2.3	40	600	640
90	Pohono Tr/McGurk Meadow Tr	6,760	7.2	3,200	840	4,040	0.1	0	40	40
128	Pohono Tr/Taft Point Tr	7,480	9.6	4,120	1,040	5,160	2.4	920	200	1,120
164	Pohono Tr/Taft Point Tr	7,680	10.2	4,320	1,040	5,360	0.6	200	0	200
224	Pohono Tr/Sentinel Dome Tr	7,760	12.0	4,800	1,440	6,240	1.8	480	400	880
260	Glacier Point Rd Crossing	7,320	12.9	4,800	1,880	6,680	0.9	0	440	440
270	Panorama Trailhead	7,280	13.0	4,800	1,920	6,720	0.1	0	40	40
266	Glacier Point Tr	7,200	13.3	4,840	2,040	6,880	0.3	40	120	160
268	Glacier Point	7,214	13.3	4,854	2,040	6,894	0.0	14	0	14
	Totals		13.3	4,854	2,040	6,894	13.3	4,854	2,040	6,894

Discovery View Overlook to Glacier Point

Publisher: O'Neill Software, P.O. Box 26111, San Francisco CA 94126 (415/398-2255)

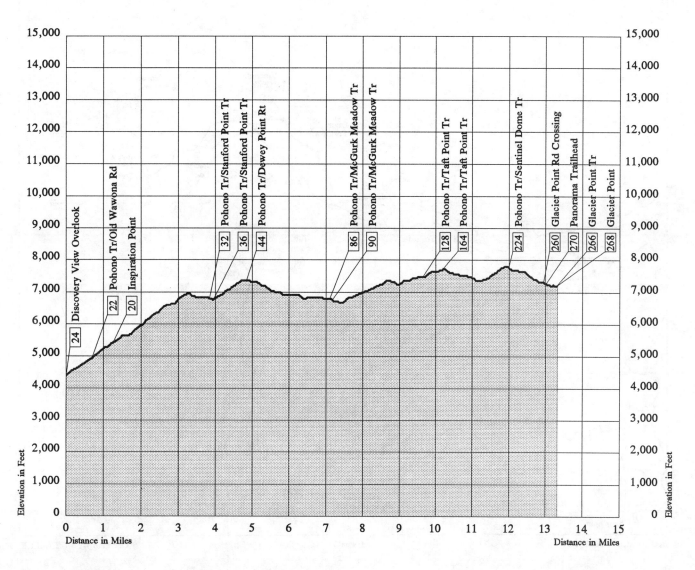

Mileage Chart

		Cumulative Distances			Incremental Distances		
Mile	Elevation	Up	Down	Rating	Up	Down	Rating
0	4,400	0	0	0	0	0	0
1	5,240	840	0	840	840	0	840
2	5,960	1,560	0	1,560	720	0	720
3	6,800	2,400	0	2,400	840	0	840
4	6,800	2,600	200	2,800	200	200	400
5	7,320	3,160	240	3,400	560	40	600
6	6,920	3,160	640	3,800	0	400	400
7	6,800	3,200	800	4,000	40	160	200
8	7,000	3,520	920	4,440	320	120	440
9	7,240	3,880	1,040	4,920	360	120	480
10	7,640	4,280	1,040	5,320	400	0	400
11	7,440	4,360	1,320	5,680	80	280	360
12	7,720	4,800	1,480	6,280	440	160	600
13	7,280	4,800	1,920	6,720	0	440	440
13.3	7,214	4,854	2,040	6,894	54	120	174
13.3	Totals	4,854	2,040	6,894	4,854	2,040	6,894

Notes

Route:

24 to 260: Pohono Trail
260 to 268: Glacier Point Trail

See 14B for opposite direction

Map Location

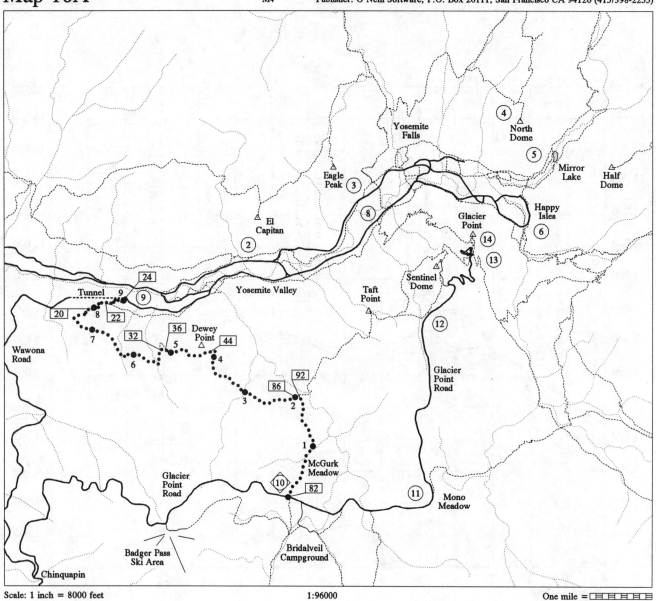

Scale: 1 inch = 8000 feet   1:96000   One mile =

Destination Chart

Num	Location	Elevation	Cumulative Distances				Incremental Distances			
			Miles	Up	Down	Total	Miles	Up	Down	Total
82	McGurk Meadow Trailhead	7,080	0.0	0	0	0	0.0	0	0	0
92	Pohono Tr/McGurk Meadow Tr	6,800	1.9	40	320	360	1.9	40	320	360
86	Pohono Tr/McGurk Meadow Tr	6,800	2.0	40	320	360	0.1	0	0	0
44	Pohono Tr/Dewey Point Rt	7,360	4.2	640	360	1,000	2.2	600	40	640
36	Pohono Tr/Stanford Point Tr	6,760	5.1	640	960	1,600	0.9	0	600	600
32	Pohono Tr/Stanford Point Tr	6,800	5.2	680	960	1,640	0.1	40	0	40
20	Inspiration Point	5,440	7.8	840	2,480	3,320	2.6	160	1,520	1,680
22	Pohono Tr/Old Wawona Rd	4,920	8.4	840	3,000	3,840	0.6	0	520	520
24	Discovery View Overlook	4,400	9.1	840	3,520	4,360	0.7	0	520	520
	Totals		9.1	840	3,520	4,360	9.1	840	3,520	4,360

McGurk Meadow Trailhead to Discovery View Overlook   10A

Publisher: O'Neill Software, P.O. Box 26111, San Francisco CA 94126 (415/398-2255)

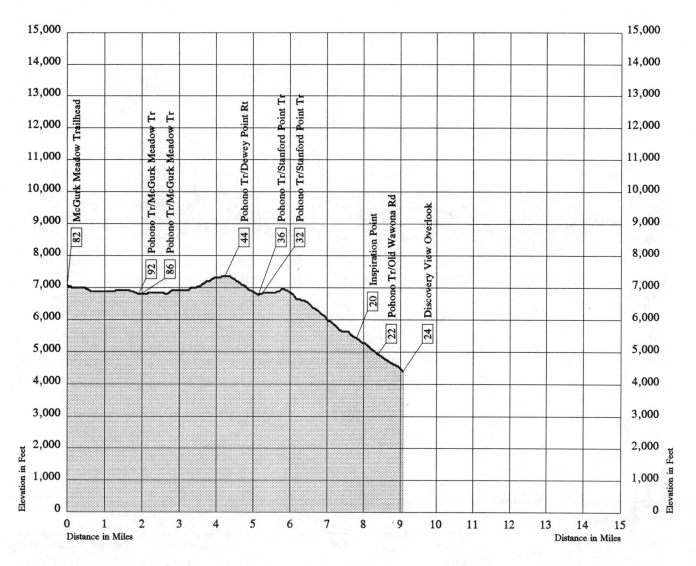

Mileage Chart

Mile	Elevation	Cumulative Distances			Incremental Distances		
		Up	Down	Rating	Up	Down	Rating
0	7,080	0	0	0	0	0	0
1	6,880	0	200	200	0	200	200
2	6,800	40	320	360	40	120	160
3	6,920	200	360	560	160	40	200
4	7,320	600	360	960	400	0	400
5	6,880	640	840	1,480	40	480	520
6	6,840	840	1,080	1,920	200	240	440
7	6,000	840	1,920	2,760	0	840	840
8	5,280	840	2,640	3,480	0	720	720
9	4,480	840	3,440	4,280	0	800	800
9.1	4,400	840	3,520	4,360	0	80	80
9.1	Totals	840	3,520	4,360	840	3,520	4,360

Notes

Route:
  82 to 86:   McGurk Meadow Trail
  86 to 24:   Pohono Trail

See 9A for opposite direction

Map Location

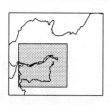

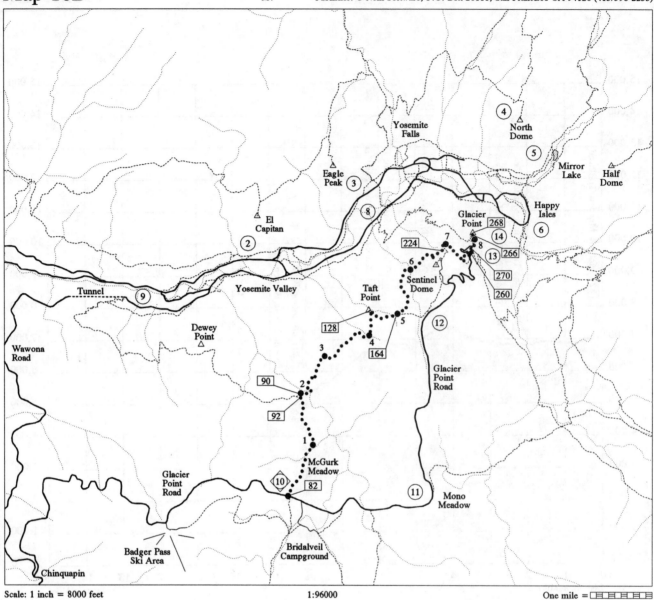

Scale: 1 inch = 8000 feet   1:96000   One mile =

Destination Chart

Num	Location	Elevation	Cumulative Distances				Incremental Distances			
			Miles	Up	Down	Total	Miles	Up	Down	Total
82	McGurk Meadow Trailhead	7,080	0.0	0	0	0	0.0	0	0	0
92	Pohono Tr/McGurk Meadow Tr	6,800	1.9	40	320	360	1.9	40	320	360
90	Pohono Tr/McGurk Meadow Tr	6,760	2.0	40	360	400	0.1	0	40	40
128	Pohono Tr/Taft Point Tr	7,480	4.5	960	560	1,520	2.5	920	200	1,120
164	Pohono Tr/Taft Point Tr	7,680	5.0	1,160	560	1,720	0.5	200	0	200
224	Pohono Tr/Sentinel Dome Tr	7,760	6.8	1,640	960	2,600	1.8	480	400	880
260	Glacier Point Rd Crossing	7,320	7.8	1,640	1,400	3,040	1.0	0	440	440
270	Panorama Trailhead	7,280	7.8	1,640	1,440	3,080	0.0	0	40	40
266	Glacier Point Tr	7,200	8.1	1,680	1,560	3,240	0.3	40	120	160
268	Glacier Point	7,214	8.1	1,694	1,560	3,254	0.0	14	0	14
	Totals		8.1	1,694	1,560	3,254	8.1	1,694	1,560	3,254

Publisher: O'Neill Software, P.O. Box 26111, San Francisco CA 94126 (415/398-2255)

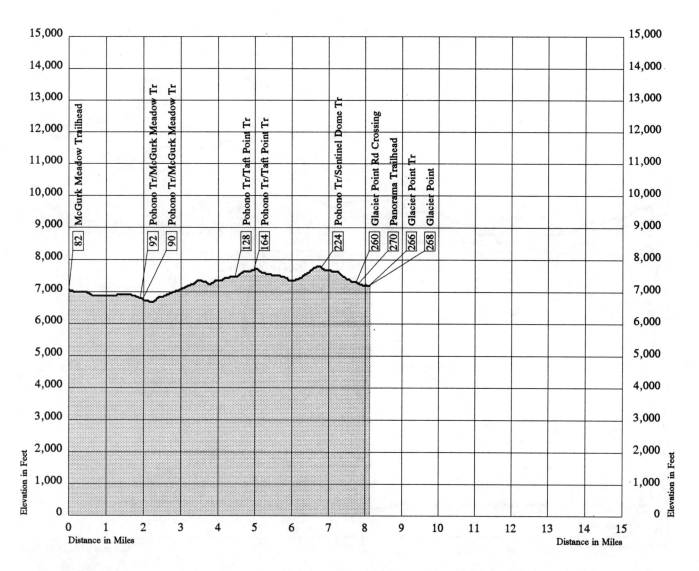

Mileage Chart

Mile	Elevation	Cumulative Distances			Incremental Distances		
		Up	Down	Rating	Up	Down	Rating
0	7,080	0	0	0	0	0	0
1	6,880	0	200	200	0	200	200
2	6,720	40	400	440	40	200	240
3	7,080	440	440	880	400	40	440
4	7,360	840	560	1,400	400	120	520
5	7,720	1,200	560	1,760	360	0	360
6	7,360	1,200	920	2,120	0	360	360
7	7,680	1,640	1,040	2,680	440	120	560
8	7,240	1,680	1,520	3,200	40	480	520
8.1	7,214	1,694	1,560	3,254	14	40	54
8.1	Totals	1,694	1,560	3,254	1,694	1,560	3,254

Notes

Route:
82 to 90:   McGurk Meadow Trail
90 to 260:   Pohono Trail
260 to 268: Glacier Point Trail

Map Location

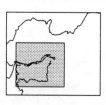

McGurk Meadow Trailhead to Glacier Point

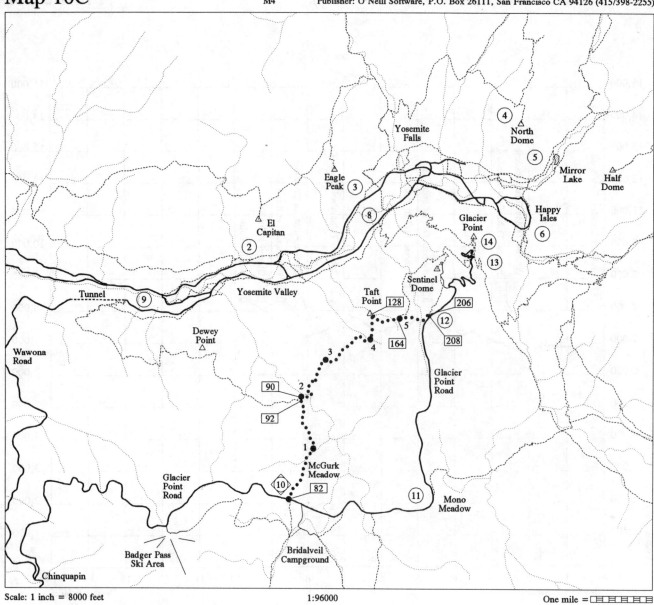

Scale: 1 inch = 8000 feet   1:96000   One mile = ▢▢▢▢▢▢

Destination Chart

Num	Location	Elevation	Cumulative Distances				Incremental Distances			
			Miles	Up	Down	Total	Miles	Up	Down	Total
82	McGurk Meadow Trailhead	7,080	0.0	0	0	0	0.0	0	0	0
92	Pohono Tr/McGurk Meadow Tr	6,800	1.9	40	320	360	1.9	40	320	360
90	Pohono Tr/McGurk Meadow Tr	6,760	2.0	40	360	400	0.1	0	40	40
128	Pohono Tr/Taft Point Tr	7,480	4.5	960	560	1,520	2.5	920	200	1,120
164	Pohono Tr/Taft Point Tr	7,680	5.0	1,160	560	1,720	0.5	200	0	200
206	Taft Point Tr/Sentinel Dome Tr	7,680	5.5	1,200	600	1,800	0.5	40	40	80
208	Taft Point Trailhead	7,720	5.6	1,240	600	1,840	0.1	40	0	40
	Totals		5.6	1,240	600	1,840	5.6	1,240	600	1,840

McGurk Meadow Trailhead to Taft Point Trailhead   10C

Publisher: O'Neill Software, P.O. Box 26111, San Francisco CA 94126 (415/398-2255)

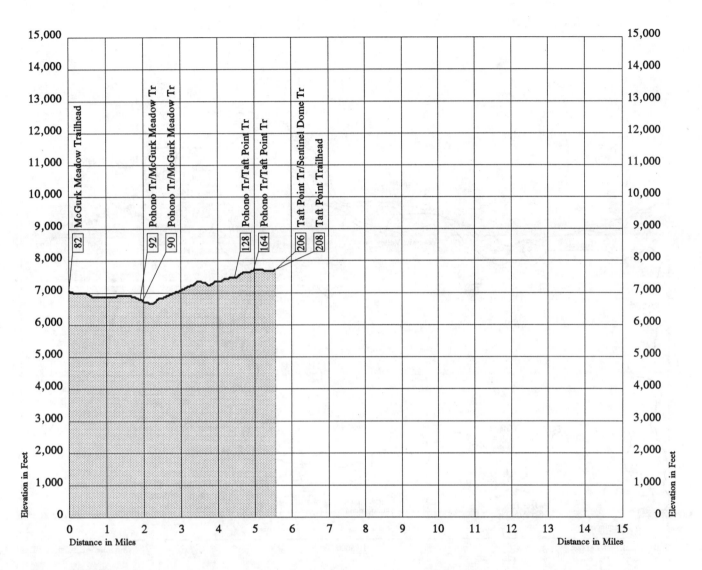

Mileage Chart

Mile	Elevation	Cumulative Distances			Incremental Distances		
		Up	Down	Rating	Up	Down	Rating
0	7,080	0	0	0	0	0	0
1	6,880	0	200	200	0	200	200
2	6,720	40	400	440	40	200	240
3	7,080	440	440	880	400	40	440
4	7,360	840	560	1,400	400	120	520
5	7,720	1,200	560	1,760	360	0	360
5.6	7,720	1,240	600	1,840	40	40	80
5.6	Totals	1,240	600	1,840	1,240	600	1,840

Notes

Route:

82 to 90:	McGurk Meadow Trail
90 to 164:	Pohono Trail
164 to 206:	Taft Point Trail
206 to 208:	Sentinel Dome Trail

See 12A for opposite direction

Map Location

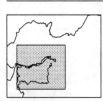

M4   Publisher: O'Neill Software, P.O. Box 26111, San Francisco CA 94126 (415/398-2255)

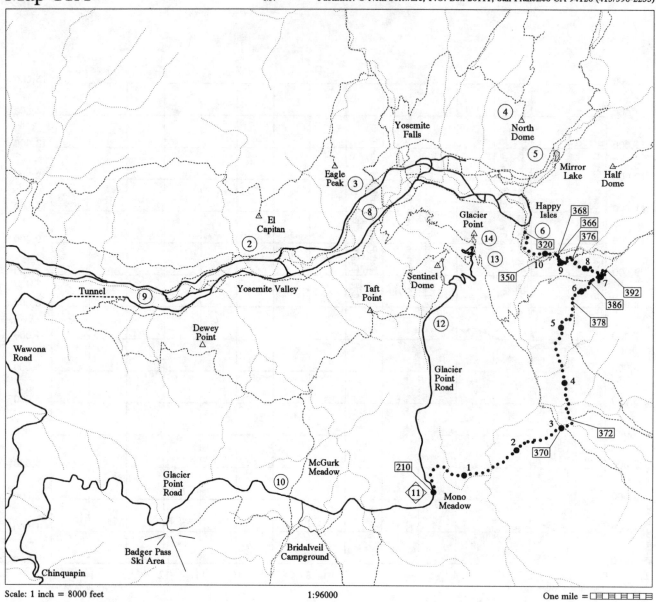

Scale: 1 inch = 8000 feet   1:96000   One mile =

Destination Chart

Num	Location	Elevation	Cumulative Distances				Incremental Distances			
			Miles	Up	Down	Total	Miles	Up	Down	Total
210	Mono Meadow Trailhead	7,240	0.0	0	0	0	0.0	0	0	0
370	Mono Meadow Tr/Buena Vista Tr	6,400	3.0	160	1,000	1,160	3.0	160	1,000	1,160
372	Mono Meadow Tr/Illilouette Creek Tr	6,400	3.3	160	1,000	1,160	0.3	0	0	0
378	Mono Meadow Tr/Merced Pass Tr	6,800	5.6	760	1,200	1,960	2.3	600	200	800
386	Panorama Tr/Mono Meadow Tr	6,600	6.4	760	1,400	2,160	0.8	0	200	200
392	John Muir Tr/Panorama Tr	6,000	7.4	760	2,000	2,760	1.0	0	600	600
376	John Muir Tr/Crossover Tr	5,480	8.4	800	2,560	3,360	1.0	40	560	600
366	John Muir Tr/Horse Tr	4,600	9.7	840	3,480	4,320	1.3	40	920	960
368	John Muir Tr/Mist Tr	4,600	9.8	840	3,480	4,320	0.1	0	0	0
350	Vernal Fall Footbridge	4,400	9.9	840	3,680	4,520	0.1	0	200	200
320	Happy Isles Trailhead	4,040	10.7	840	4,040	4,880	0.8	0	360	360
	Totals		10.7	840	4,040	4,880	10.7	840	4,040	4,880

Mono Meadow Trailhead to Happy Isles Trailhead   11A

Publisher: O'Neill Software, P.O. Box 26111, San Francisco CA 94126 (415/398-2255)

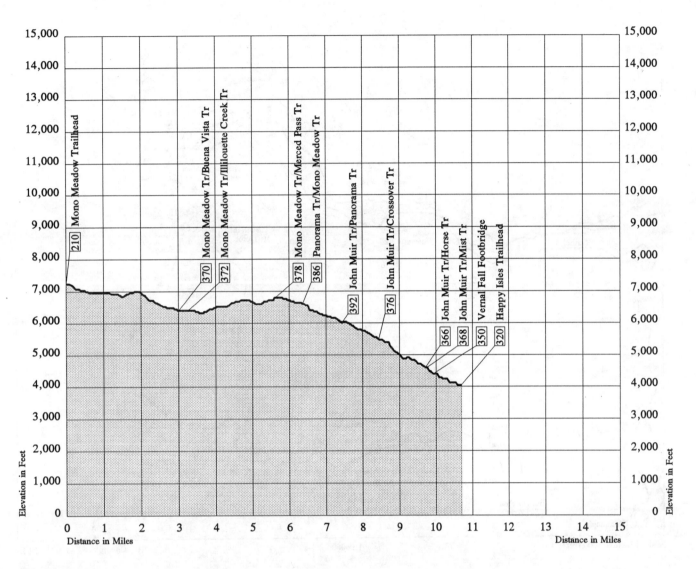

Mileage Chart

		Cumulative Distances			Incremental Distances		
Mile	Elevation	Up	Down	Rating	Up	Down	Rating
0	7,240	0	0	0	0	0	0
1	6,960	0	280	280	0	280	280
2	6,960	160	440	600	160	160	320
3	6,400	160	1,000	1,160	0	560	560
4	6,480	320	1,080	1,400	160	80	240
5	6,680	560	1,120	1,680	240	40	280
6	6,720	760	1,280	2,040	200	160	360
7	6,240	760	1,760	2,520	0	480	480
8	5,760	800	2,280	3,080	40	520	560
9	5,000	800	3,040	3,840	0	760	760
10	4,400	840	3,680	4,520	40	640	680
10.7	4,040	840	4,040	4,880	0	360	360
10.7	Totals	840	4,040	4,880	840	4,040	4,880

Notes

Route:

210 to 386:	Mono Meadow Trail
386 to 392:	Panorama Trail
392 to 320:	John Muir Trail

Map Location

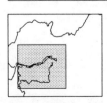

Mono Meadow Trailhead to Happy Isles Trailhead

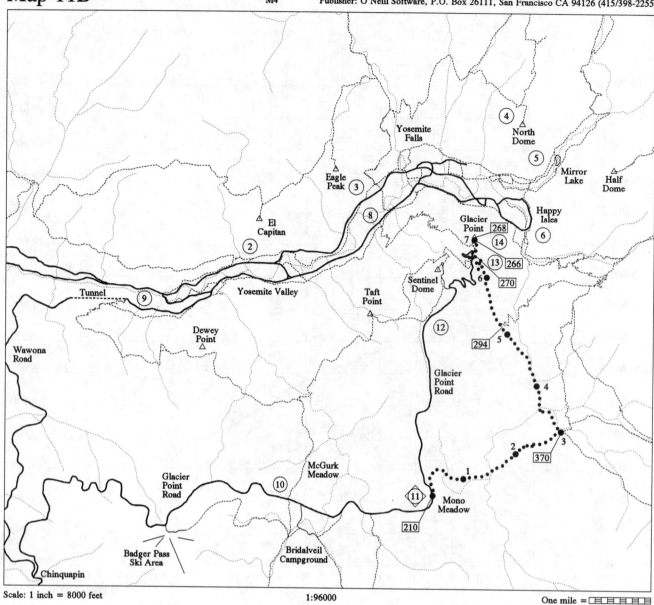

Scale: 1 inch = 8000 feet   1:96000   One mile =

Destination Chart

Num	Location	Elevation	Cumulative Distances				Incremental Distances			
			Miles	Up	Down	Total	Miles	Up	Down	Total
210	Mono Meadow Trailhead	7,240	0.0	0	0	0	0.0	0	0	0
370	Mono Meadow Tr/Buena Vista Tr	6,400	3.0	160	1,000	1,160	3.0	160	1,000	1,160
294	Panorama Tr/Buena Vista Tr	6,440	5.1	520	1,320	1,840	2.1	360	320	680
270	Panorama Trailhead	7,280	6.7	1,360	1,320	2,680	1.6	840	0	840
266	Glacier Point Tr	7,200	7.0	1,400	1,440	2,840	0.3	40	120	160
268	Glacier Point	7,214	7.0	1,414	1,440	2,854	0.0	14	0	14
	Totals		7.0	1,414	1,440	2,854	7.0	1,414	1,440	2,854

Mono Meadow Trailhead to Glacier Point

11B

Publisher: O'Neill Software, P.O. Box 26111, San Francisco CA 94126 (415/398-2255)

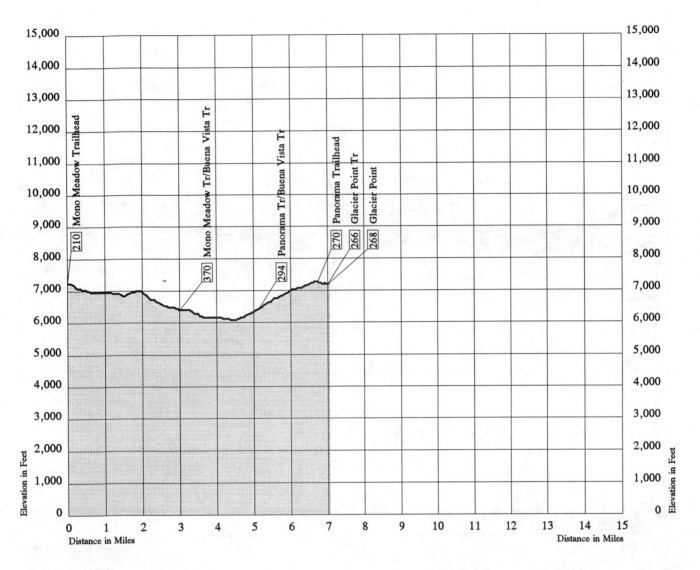

Mileage Chart

		Cumulative Distances			Incremental Distances		
Mile	Elevation	Up	Down	Rating	Up	Down	Rating
0	7,240	0	0	0	0	0	0
1	6,960	0	280	280	0	280	280
2	6,960	160	440	600	160	160	320
3	6,400	160	1,000	1,160	0	560	560
4	6,160	160	1,240	1,400	0	240	240
5	6,360	440	1,320	1,760	280	80	360
6	7,000	1,080	1,320	2,400	640	0	640
7	7,200	1,400	1,440	2,840	320	120	440
7.0	7,214	1,414	1,440	2,854	14	0	14
7.0	Totals	1,414	1,440	2,854	1,414	1,440	2,854

Notes

Route:

210 to 370:	Mono Meadow Trail
370 to 294:	Buena Vista Trail
294 to 270:	Panorama Trail
270 to 268:	Glacier Point Trail

Map Location

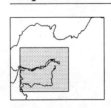

Mono Meadow Trailhead to Glacier Point

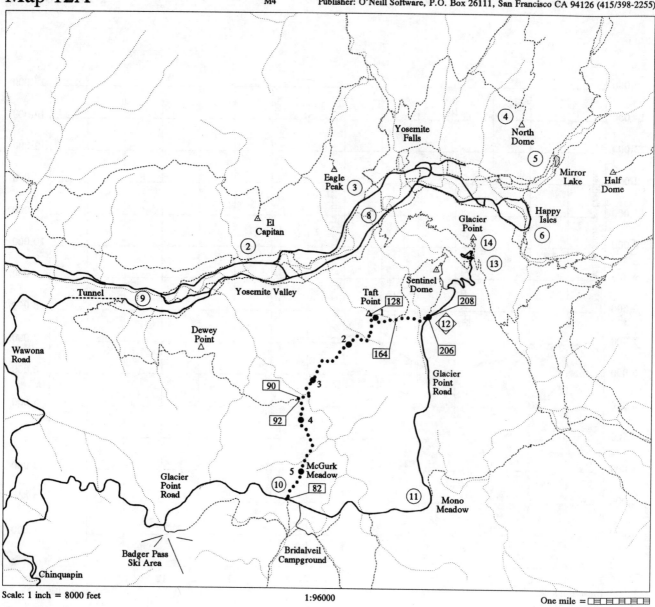

Scale: 1 inch = 8000 feet   1:96000   One mile = ▭▭▭▭▭▭

Destination Chart

Num	Location	Elevation	Cumulative Distances				Incremental Distances			
			Miles	Up	Down	Total	Miles	Up	Down	Total
208	Taft Point Trailhead	7,720	0.0	0	0	0	0.0	0	0	0
206	Taft Point Tr/Sentinel Dome Tr	7,680	0.0	0	40	40	0.0	0	40	40
164	Pohono Tr/Taft Point Tr	7,680	0.6	40	80	120	0.6	40	40	80
128	Pohono Tr/Taft Point Tr	7,480	1.1	40	280	320	0.5	0	200	200
90	Pohono Tr/McGurk Meadow Tr	6,760	3.6	240	1,200	1,440	2.5	200	920	1,120
92	Pohono Tr/McGurk Meadow Tr	6,800	3.6	280	1,200	1,480	0.0	40	0	40
82	McGurk Meadow Trailhead	7,080	5.6	600	1,240	1,840	2.0	320	40	360
	Totals		5.6	600	1,240	1,840	5.6	600	1,240	1,840

Taft Point Trailhead to McGurk Meadow Trailhead   12A

Publisher: O'Neill Software, P.O. Box 26111, San Francisco CA 94126 (415/398-2255)

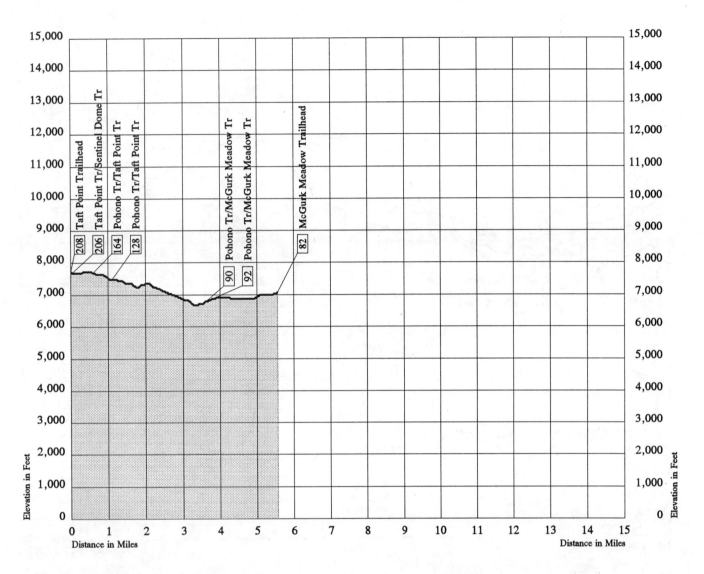

Mileage Chart

Mile	Elevation	Cumulative Distances			Incremental Distances		
		Up	Down	Rating	Up	Down	Rating
0	7,720	0	0	0	0	0	0
1	7,520	40	240	280	40	240	280
2	7,360	160	520	680	120	280	400
3	6,880	160	1,000	1,160	0	480	480
4	6,920	400	1,200	1,600	240	200	440
5	6,960	480	1,240	1,720	80	40	120
5.6	7,080	600	1,240	1,840	120	0	120
5.6	Totals	600	1,240	1,840	600	1,240	1,840

Notes

Route:
  208 to 206:   Sentinel Dome Trail
  206 to 164:   Taft Point Trail
  164 to 90:   Pohono Trail
  90 to 82:   McGurk Meadow Trail

See 10C for opposite direction

Map Location

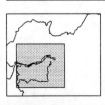

Taft Point Trailhead to McGurk Meadow Trailhead

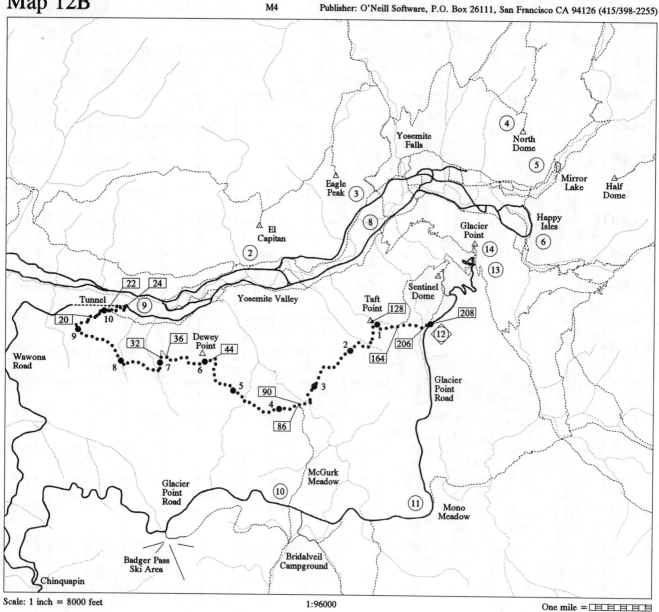

Scale: 1 inch = 8000 feet   1:96000   One mile =

Destination Chart

Num	Location	Elevation	Cumulative Distances				Incremental Distances			
			Miles	Up	Down	Total	Miles	Up	Down	Total
208	Taft Point Trailhead	7,720	0.0	0	0	0	0.0	0	0	0
206	Taft Point Tr/Sentinel Dome Tr	7,680	0.0	0	40	40	0.0	0	40	40
164	Pohono Tr/Taft Point Tr	7,680	0.6	40	80	120	0.6	40	40	80
128	Pohono Tr/Taft Point Tr	7,480	1.1	40	280	320	0.5	0	200	200
90	Pohono Tr/McGurk Meadow Tr	6,760	3.6	240	1,200	1,440	2.5	200	920	1,120
86	Pohono Tr/McGurk Meadow Tr	6,800	3.7	280	1,200	1,480	0.1	40	0	40
44	Pohono Tr/Dewey Point Rt	7,360	5.9	880	1,240	2,120	2.2	600	40	640
36	Pohono Tr/Stanford Point Tr	6,760	6.8	880	1,840	2,720	0.9	0	600	600
32	Pohono Tr/Stanford Point Tr	6,800	6.9	920	1,840	2,760	0.1	40	0	40
20	Inspiration Point	5,440	9.5	1,080	3,360	4,440	2.6	160	1,520	1,680
22	Pohono Tr/Old Wawona Rd	4,920	10.1	1,080	3,880	4,960	0.6	0	520	520
24	Discovery View Overlook	4,400	10.8	1,080	4,400	5,480	0.7	0	520	520
	Totals		10.8	1,080	4,400	5,480	10.8	1,080	4,400	5,480

Taft Point Trailhead to Discovery View Overlook

12B

Publisher: O'Neill Software, P.O. Box 26111, San Francisco CA 94126 (415/398-2255)

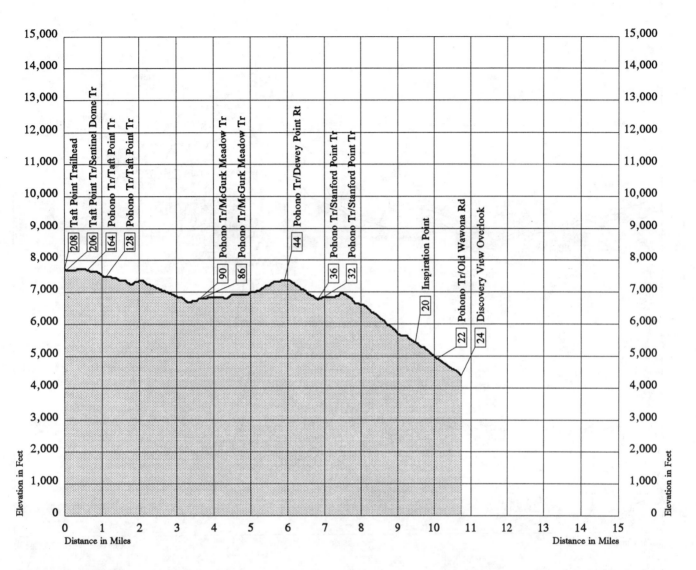

Mileage Chart

Mile	Elevation	Cumulative Distances			Incremental Distances		
		Up	Down	Rating	Up	Down	Rating
0	7,720	0	0	0	0	0	0
1	7,520	40	240	280	40	240	280
2	7,360	160	520	680	120	280	400
3	6,880	160	1,000	1,160	0	480	480
4	6,840	320	1,200	1,520	160	200	360
5	7,000	520	1,240	1,760	200	40	240
6	7,360	880	1,240	2,120	360	0	360
7	6,840	960	1,840	2,800	80	600	680
8	6,600	1,080	2,200	3,280	120	360	480
9	5,680	1,080	3,120	4,200	0	920	920
10	5,000	1,080	3,800	4,880	0	680	680
10.8	4,400	1,080	4,400	5,480	0	600	600
10.8	Totals	1,080	4,400	5,480	1,080	4,400	5,480

Notes

Route:

208 to 206:	Sentinel Dome Trail
206 to 164:	Taft Point Trail
164 to 24:	Pohono Trail

Map Location

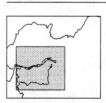

Taft Point Trailhead to Discovery View Overlook

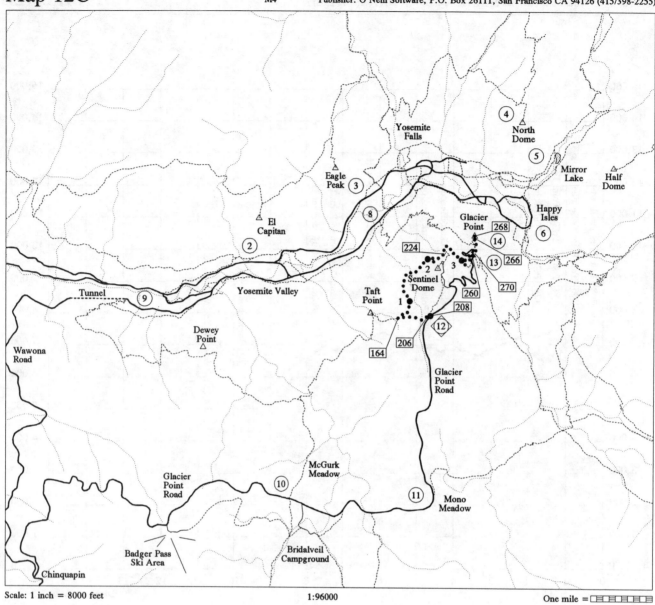

Scale: 1 inch = 8000 feet   1:96000   One mile =

Destination Chart

Num	Location	Elevation	Cumulative Distances				Incremental Distances			
			Miles	Up	Down	Total	Miles	Up	Down	Total
208	Taft Point Trailhead	7,720	0.0	0	0	0	0.0	0	0	0
206	Taft Point Tr/Sentinel Dome Tr	7,680	0.0	0	40	40	0.0	0	40	40
164	Pohono Tr/Taft Point Tr	7,680	0.6	40	80	120	0.6	40	40	80
224	Pohono Tr/Sentinel Dome Tr	7,760	2.4	520	480	1,000	1.8	480	400	880
260	Glacier Point Rd Crossing	7,320	3.4	520	920	1,440	1.0	0	440	440
270	Panorama Trailhead	7,280	3.5	520	960	1,480	0.1	0	40	40
266	Glacier Point Tr	7,200	3.7	560	1,080	1,640	0.2	40	120	160
268	Glacier Point	7,214	3.8	574	1,080	1,654	0.1	14	0	14
	Totals		3.8	574	1,080	1,654	3.8	574	1,080	1,654

Taft Point Trailhead to Glacier Point

12C

Publisher: O'Neill Software, P.O. Box 26111, San Francisco CA 94126 (415/398-2255)

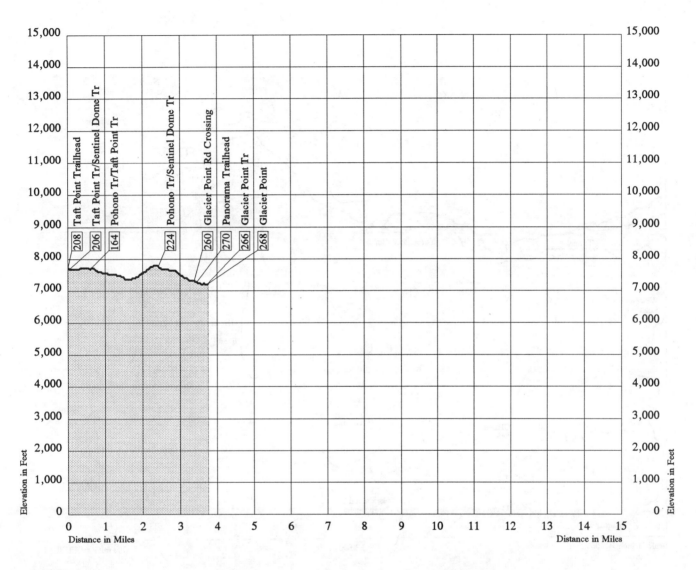

Mileage Chart

		Cumulative Distances			Incremental Distances		
Mile	Elevation	Up	Down	Rating	Up	Down	Rating
0	7,720	0	0	0	0	0	0
1	7,560	80	240	320	80	240	320
2	7,560	280	440	720	200	200	400
3	7,480	520	760	1,280	240	320	560
3.8	7,214	574	1,080	1,654	54	320	374
3.8	Totals	574	1,080	1,654	574	1,080	1,654

Notes

Route:

208 to 206:	Sentinel Dome Trail
206 to 164:	Taft Point Trail
164 to 260:	Pohono Trail
260 to 268:	Glacier Point Trail

Map Location

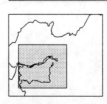

Taft Point Trailhead to Glacier Point

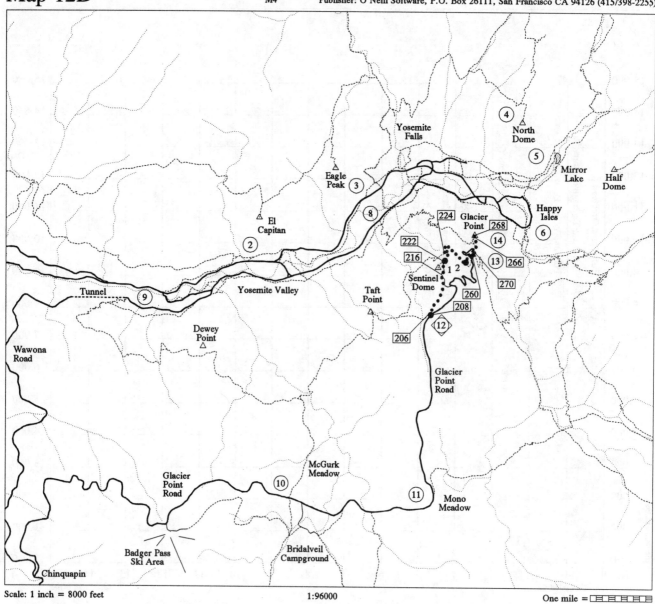

Scale: 1 inch = 8000 feet   1:96000   One mile =

Destination Chart

Num	Location	Elevation	Cumulative Distances				Incremental Distances			
			Miles	Up	Down	Total	Miles	Up	Down	Total
208	Taft Point Trailhead	7,720	0.0	0	0	0	0.0	0	0	0
206	Taft Point Tr/Sentinel Dome Tr	7,680	0.0	0	40	40	0.0	0	40	40
216	Sentinel Dome Tr/Sentinel Dome Rd	7,840	0.7	200	80	280	0.7	200	40	240
222	Sentinel Dome Tr/Sentinel Dome Rd	7,960	1.0	320	80	400	0.3	120	0	120
224	Pohono Tr/Sentinel Dome Tr	7,760	1.3	320	280	600	0.3	0	200	200
260	Glacier Point Rd Crossing	7,320	2.2	320	720	1,040	0.9	0	440	440
270	Panorama Trailhead	7,280	2.3	320	760	1,080	0.1	0	40	40
266	Glacier Point Tr	7,200	2.6	360	880	1,240	0.3	40	120	160
268	Glacier Point	7,214	2.6	374	880	1,254	0.0	14	0	14
	Totals		2.6	374	880	1,254	2.6	374	880	1,254

Publisher: O'Neill Software, P.O. Box 26111, San Francisco CA 94126 (415/398-2255)

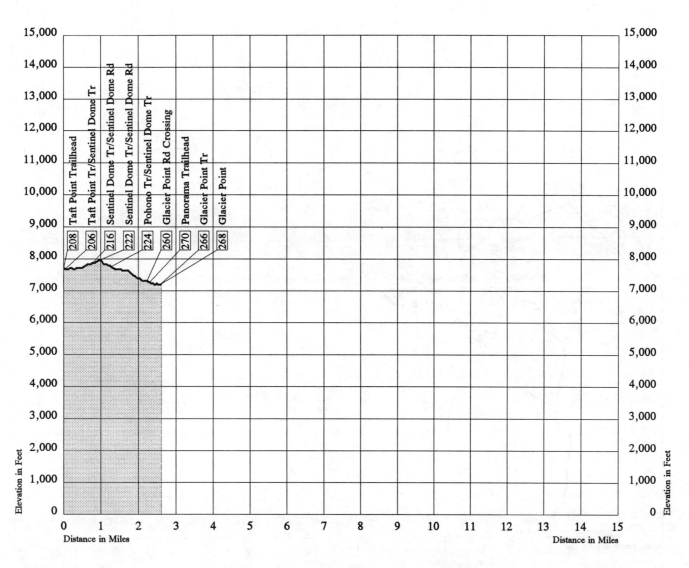

Mileage Chart

Mile	Elevation	Cumulative Distances			Incremental Distances		
		Up	Down	Rating	Up	Down	Rating
0	7,720	0	0	0	0	0	0
1	7,960	320	80	400	320	80	400
2	7,400	320	640	960	0	560	560
2.6	7,214	374	880	1,254	54	240	294
2.6	Totals	374	880	1,254	374	880	1,254

Notes

Route:
 208 to 216: Sentinel Dome Trail
 216 to 222: Sentinel Dome Road
 222 to 224: Sentinel Dome Trail
 224 to 260: Pohono Trail
 260 to 268: Glacier Point Trail

Trail from 206 to 224 not measured

Map Location

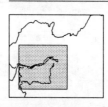

Taft Point Trailhead to Glacier Point

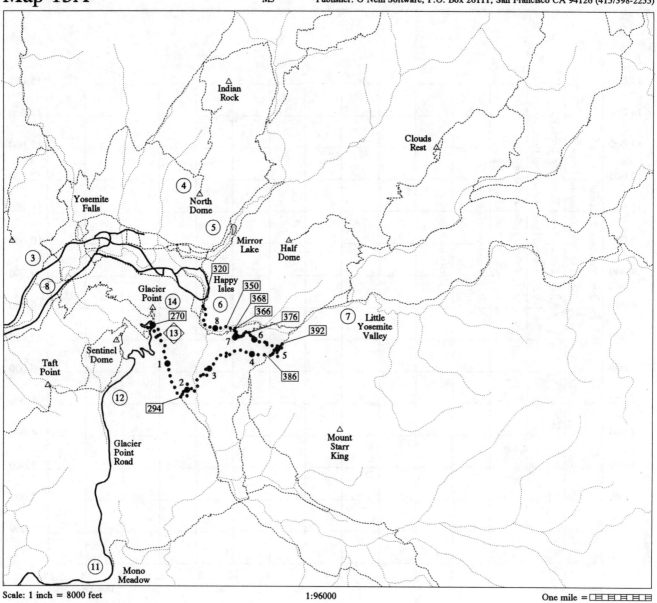

Scale: 1 inch = 8000 feet   1:96000   One mile =

Destination Chart

Num	Location	Elevation	Cumulative Distances				Incremental Distances			
			Miles	Up	Down	Total	Miles	Up	Down	Total
270	Panorama Trailhead	7,280	0.0	0	0	0	0.0	0	0	0
294	Panorama Tr/Buena Vista Tr	6,440	1.6	0	840	840	1.6	0	840	840
386	Panorama Tr/Mono Meadow Tr	6,600	4.2	720	1,400	2,120	2.6	720	560	1,280
392	John Muir Tr/Panorama Tr	6,000	5.3	720	2,000	2,720	1.1	0	600	600
376	John Muir Tr/Crossover Tr	5,480	6.3	760	2,560	3,320	1.0	40	560	600
366	John Muir Tr/Horse Tr	4,600	7.6	800	3,480	4,280	1.3	40	920	960
368	John Muir Tr/Mist Tr	4,600	7.6	800	3,480	4,280	0.0	0	0	0
350	Vernal Fall Footbridge	4,400	7.8	800	3,680	4,480	0.2	0	200	200
320	Happy Isles Trailhead	4,040	8.6	800	4,040	4,840	0.8	0	360	360
		Totals	8.6	800	4,040	4,840	8.6	800	4,040	4,840

Publisher: O'Neill Software, P.O. Box 26111, San Francisco CA 94126 (415/398-2255)

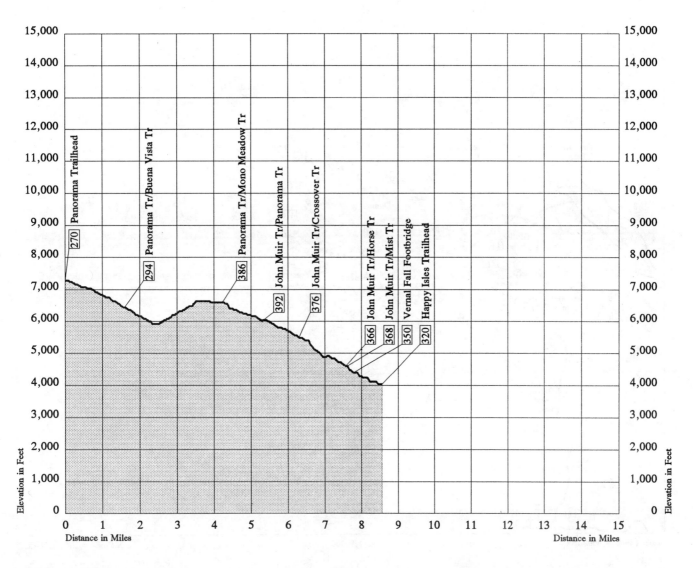

Mileage Chart

		Cumulative Distances			Incremental Distances		
Mile	Elevation	Up	Down	Rating	Up	Down	Rating
0	7,280	0	0	0	0	0	0
1	6,840	0	440	440	0	440	440
2	6,160	0	1,120	1,120	0	680	680
3	6,280	360	1,360	1,720	360	240	600
4	6,600	720	1,400	2,120	360	40	400
5	6,160	720	1,840	2,560	0	440	440
6	5,680	760	2,360	3,120	40	520	560
7	4,880	760	3,160	3,920	0	800	800
8	4,280	800	3,800	4,600	40	640	680
8.6	4,040	800	4,040	4,840	0	240	240
8.6	Totals	800	4,040	4,840	800	4,040	4,840

Notes

Route:
270 to 392: Panorama Trail
392 to 320: John Muir Trail

See 6E for opposite direction (to 286)

Map Location

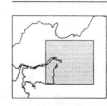

Panorama Trailhead to Happy Isles Trailhead

M5   Publisher: O'Neill Software, P.O. Box 26111, San Francisco CA 94126 (415/398-2255)

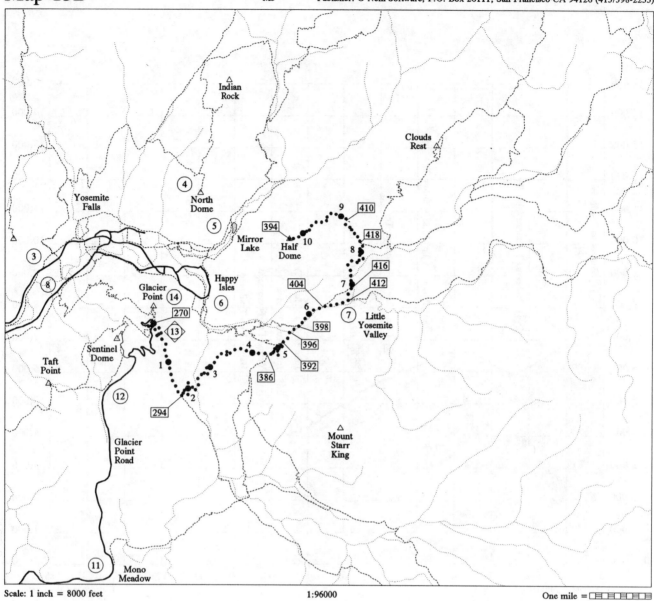

Scale: 1 inch = 8000 feet   1:96000   One mile = ☐☐☐☐☐☐

Destination Chart

Num	Location	Elevation	Cumulative Distances				Incremental Distances			
			Miles	Up	Down	Total	Miles	Up	Down	Total
270	Panorama Trailhead	7,280	0.0	0	0	0	0.0	0	0	0
294	Panorama Tr/Buena Vista Tr	6,440	1.6	0	840	840	1.6	0	840	840
386	Panorama Tr/Mono Meadow Tr	6,600	4.2	720	1,400	2,120	2.6	720	560	1,280
392	John Muir Tr/Panorama Tr	6,000	5.3	720	2,000	2,720	1.1	0	600	600
396	Nevada Fall Footbridge	5,960	5.5	720	2,040	2,760	0.2	0	40	40
398	John Muir Tr/Mist Tr	5,960	5.7	720	2,040	2,760	0.2	0	0	0
404	John Muir Tr/LYV Bypass	6,120	6.3	920	2,080	3,000	0.6	200	40	240
412	Little Yosemite Valley	6,120	6.7	920	2,080	3,000	0.4	0	0	0
416	John Muir Tr/LYV Bypass	6,120	6.9	920	2,080	3,000	0.2	0	0	0
418	Half Dome Tr/John Muir Tr	7,000	8.3	1,800	2,080	3,880	1.4	880	0	880
410	Tr to Spring	7,400	8.9	2,200	2,080	4,280	0.6	400	0	400
394	Half Dome	8,836	10.3	3,676	2,120	5,796	1.4	1,476	40	1,516
	Totals		10.3	3,676	2,120	5,796	10.3	3,676	2,120	5,796

Panorama Trailhead to Half Dome

Publisher: O'Neill Software, P.O. Box 26111, San Francisco CA 94126 (415/398-2255)

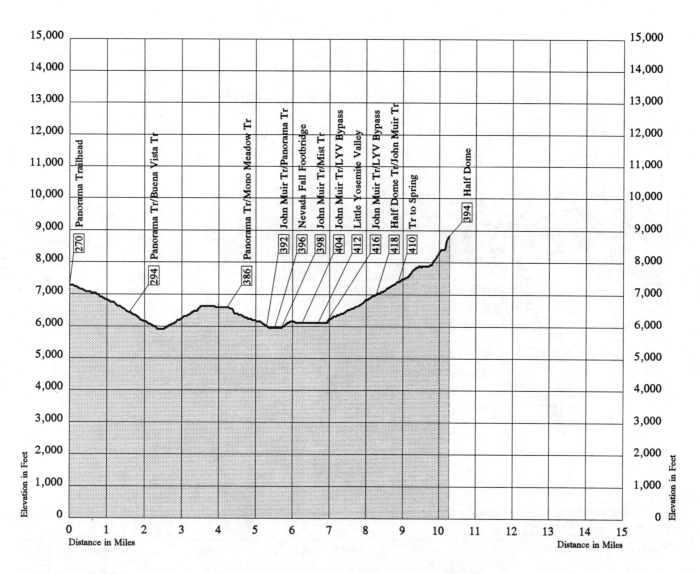

Mileage Chart

Mile	Elevation	Cumulative Distances			Incremental Distances		
		Up	Down	Rating	Up	Down	Rating
0	7,280	0	0	0	0	0	0
1	6,840	0	440	440	0	440	440
2	6,160	0	1,120	1,120	0	680	680
3	6,280	360	1,360	1,720	360	240	600
4	6,600	720	1,400	2,120	360	40	400
5	6,160	720	1,840	2,560	0	440	440
6	6,160	920	2,040	2,960	200	200	400
7	6,240	1,040	2,080	3,120	120	40	160
8	6,840	1,640	2,080	3,720	600	0	600
9	7,480	2,280	2,080	4,360	640	0	640
10	8,320	3,160	2,120	5,280	880	40	920
10.3	8,836	3,676	2,120	5,796	516	0	516
10.3	Totals	3,676	2,120	5,796	3,676	2,120	5,796

Notes

Route:

270 to 392:	Panorama Trail
392 to 418:	John Muir Trail
418 to 394:	Half Dome Trail

Map Location

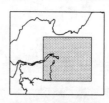

Panorama Trailhead to Half Dome

M5   Publisher: O'Neill Software, P.O. Box 26111, San Francisco CA 94126 (415/398-2255)

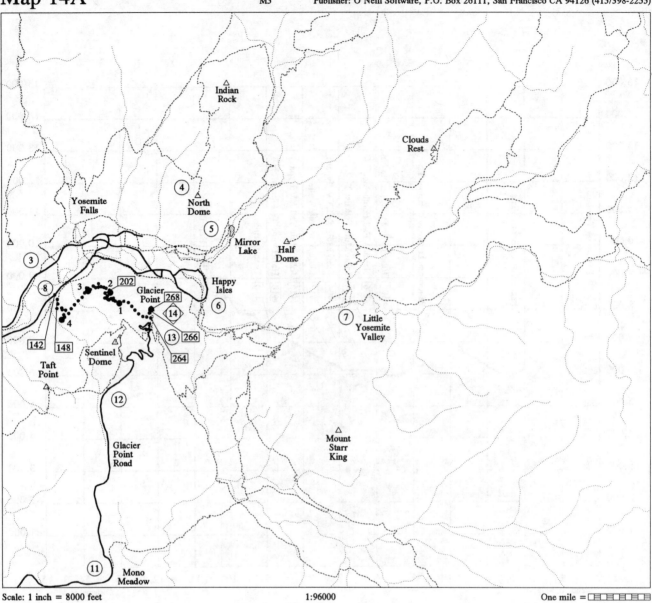

Scale: 1 inch = 8000 feet   1:96000   One mile =

Destination Chart

Num	Location	Elevation	Cumulative Distances				Incremental Distances			
			Miles	Up	Down	Total	Miles	Up	Down	Total
268	Glacier Point	7,214	0.0	0	0	0	0.0	0	0	0
266	Glacier Point Tr	7,200	0.0	0	14	14	0.0	0	14	14
264	Four Mile Tr/Glacier Point Tr	7,160	0.2	0	54	54	0.2	0	40	40
202	Union Point	6,360	1.9	0	854	854	1.7	0	800	800
148	Four Mile Tr/Valley Tr	4,000	4.7	0	3,214	3,214	2.8	0	2,360	2,360
142	Four Mile Trailhead	4,000	4.8	0	3,214	3,214	0.1	0	0	0
		Totals	4.8	0	3,214	3,214	4.8	0	3,214	3,214

Glacier Point to Four Mile Trailhead

Publisher: O'Neill Software, P.O. Box 26111, San Francisco CA 94126 (415/398-2255)

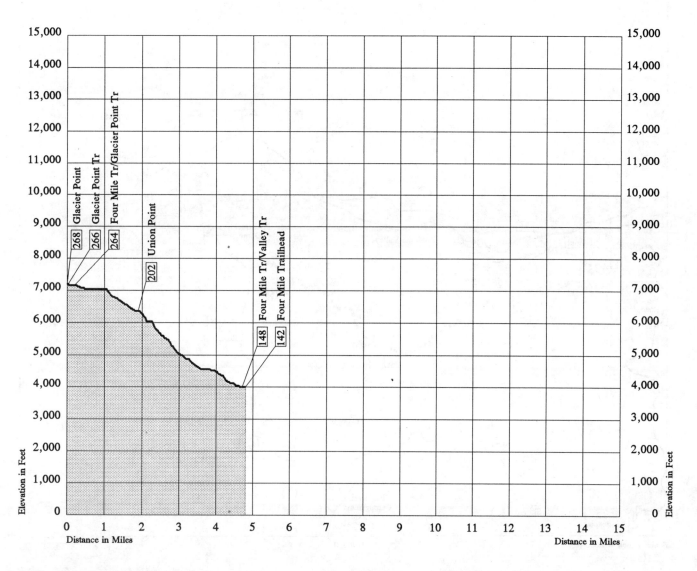

Mileage Chart

Mile	Elevation	Cumulative Distances			Incremental Distances		
		Up	Down	Rating	Up	Down	Rating
0	7,214	0	0	0	0	0	0
1	7,040	0	174	174	0	174	174
2	6,280	0	934	934	0	760	760
3	5,040	0	2,174	2,174	0	1,240	1,240
4	4,480	0	2,734	2,734	0	560	560
4.8	4,000	0	3,214	3,214	0	480	480
4.8	Totals	0	3,214	3,214	0	3,214	3,214

Notes

Route:
   268 to 264:   Glacier Point Trail
   264 to 142:   Four Mile Trail

See 8A for opposite direction

Map Location

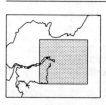

M4   Publisher: O'Neill Software, P.O. Box 26111, San Francisco CA 94126 (415/398-2255)

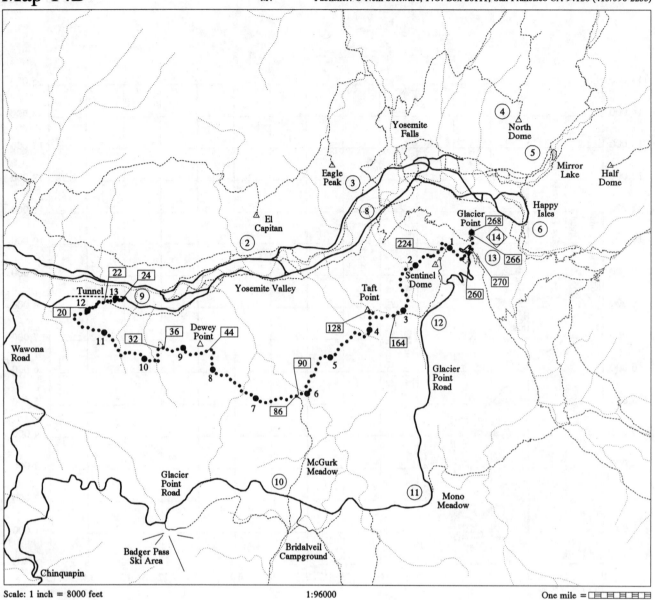

Scale: 1 inch = 8000 feet   1:96000   One mile = ▭▭▭▭▭▭

Destination Chart

Num	Location	Elevation	Cumulative Distances				Incremental Distances			
			Miles	Up	Down	Total	Miles	Up	Down	Total
268	Glacier Point	7,214	0.0	0	0	0	0.0	0	0	0
266	Glacier Point Tr	7,200	0.0	0	14	14	0.0	0	14	14
270	Panorama Trailhead	7,280	0.3	120	54	174	0.3	120	40	160
260	Glacier Point Rd Crossing	7,320	0.4	160	54	214	0.1	40	0	40
224	Pohono Tr/Sentinel Dome Tr	7,760	1.3	600	54	654	0.9	440	0	440
164	Pohono Tr/Taft Point Tr	7,680	3.2	1,000	534	1,534	1.9	400	480	880
128	Pohono Tr/Taft Point Tr	7,480	3.7	1,000	734	1,734	0.5	0	200	200
90	Pohono Tr/McGurk Meadow Tr	6,760	6.2	1,200	1,654	2,854	2.5	200	920	1,120
86	Pohono Tr/McGurk Meadow Tr	6,800	6.2	1,240	1,654	2,894	0.0	40	0	40
44	Pohono Tr/Dewey Point Rt	7,360	8.5	1,840	1,694	3,534	2.3	600	40	640
36	Pohono Tr/Stanford Point Tr	6,760	9.4	1,840	2,294	4,134	0.9	0	600	600
32	Pohono Tr/Stanford Point Tr	6,800	9.5	1,880	2,294	4,174	0.1	40	0	40
20	Inspiration Point	5,440	12.1	2,040	3,814	5,854	2.6	160	1,520	1,680
22	Pohono Tr/Old Wawona Rd	4,920	12.6	2,040	4,334	6,374	0.5	0	520	520
24	Discovery View Overlook	4,400	13.3	2,040	4,854	6,894	0.7	0	520	520
	Totals		13.3	2,040	4,854	6,894	13.3	2,040	4,854	6,894

Glacier Point to Discovery View Overlook

Publisher: O'Neill Software, P.O. Box 26111, San Francisco CA 94126 (415/398-2255)

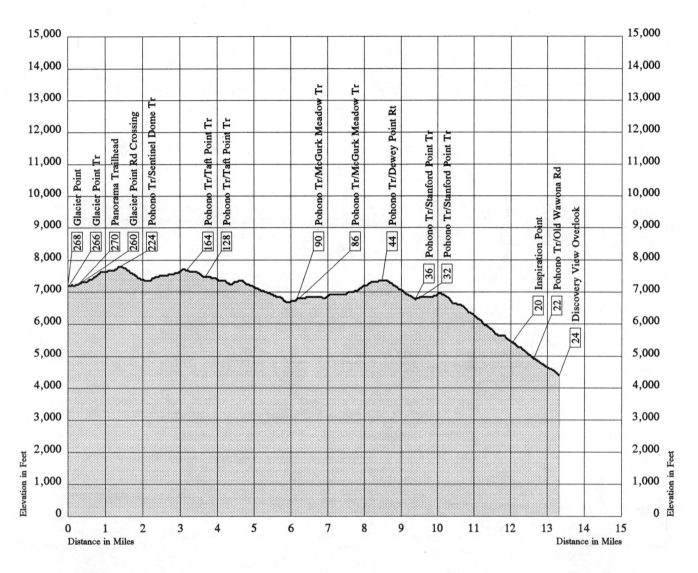

Mileage Chart

Mile	Elevation	Cumulative Distances			Incremental Distances		
		Up	Down	Rating	Up	Down	Rating
0	7,214	0	0	0	0	0	0
1	7,640	480	54	534	480	54	534
2	7,400	640	454	1,094	160	400	560
3	7,640	920	494	1,414	280	40	320
4	7,400	1,000	814	1,814	80	320	400
5	7,160	1,120	1,174	2,294	120	360	480
6	6,720	1,160	1,654	2,814	40	480	520
7	6,880	1,360	1,694	3,054	200	40	240
8	7,200	1,680	1,694	3,374	320	0	320
9	7,080	1,840	1,974	3,814	160	280	440
10	6,960	2,040	2,294	4,334	200	320	520
11	6,280	2,040	2,974	5,014	0	680	680
12	5,440	2,040	3,814	5,854	0	840	840
13	4,640	2,040	4,614	6,654	0	800	800
13.3	4,400	2,040	4,854	6,894	0	240	240
13.3	Totals	2,040	4,854	6,894	2,040	4,854	6,894

Notes

Route:
   268 to 260:   Glacier Point Trail
   260 to 24:   Pohono Trail

See 9B for opposite direction

Map Location

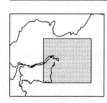

Glacier Point to Discovery View Overlook

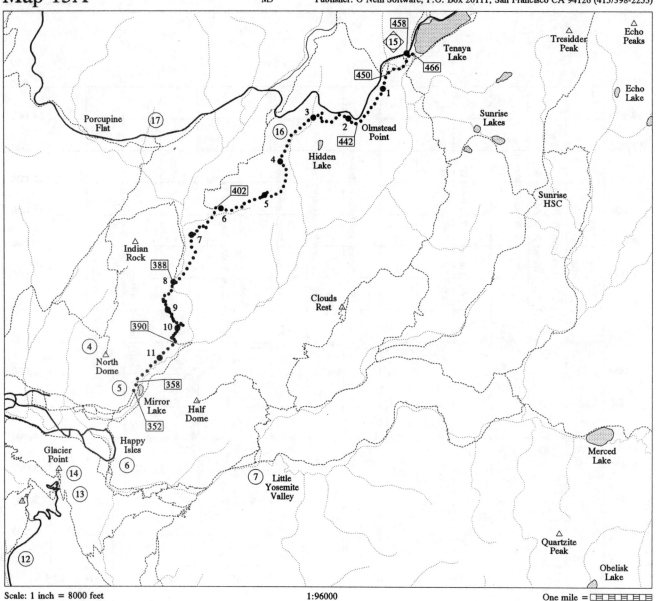

Scale: 1 inch = 8000 feet   1:96000   One mile =

Destination Chart

Num	Location	Elevation	Cumulative Distances				Incremental Distances			
			Miles	Up	Down	Total	Miles	Up	Down	Total
458	Tenaya Lake Trailhead	8,200	0.0	0	0	0	0.0	0	0	0
466	Tenaya Lake CG	8,160	0.1	0	40	40	0.1	0	40	40
450	Tenaya Lake Tr/Tr to Tioga Road	8,200	0.8	40	40	80	0.7	40	0	40
442	Olmstead Point	8,360	1.8	200	40	240	1.0	160	0	160
402	Snow Creek Tr/Tenaya Lake Tr	7,680	6.1	600	1,120	1,720	4.3	400	1,080	1,480
388	Snow Creek Tr/Indian Ridge Tr	6,720	8.0	640	2,120	2,760	1.9	40	1,000	1,040
390	Snow Creek Tr/Mirror Mdw Tr	4,120	10.6	640	4,720	5,360	2.6	0	2,600	2,600
358	Mirror Mdw Tr/Mirror Lake Tr	4,120	11.6	640	4,720	5,360	1.0	0	0	0
352	Mirror Lake Trailhead	4,120	11.7	640	4,720	5,360	0.1	0	0	0
	Totals		11.7	640	4,720	5,360	11.7	640	4,720	5,360

Tenaya Lake Trailhead to Mirror Lake Trailhead   15A

Publisher: O'Neill Software, P.O. Box 26111, San Francisco CA 94126 (415/398-2255)

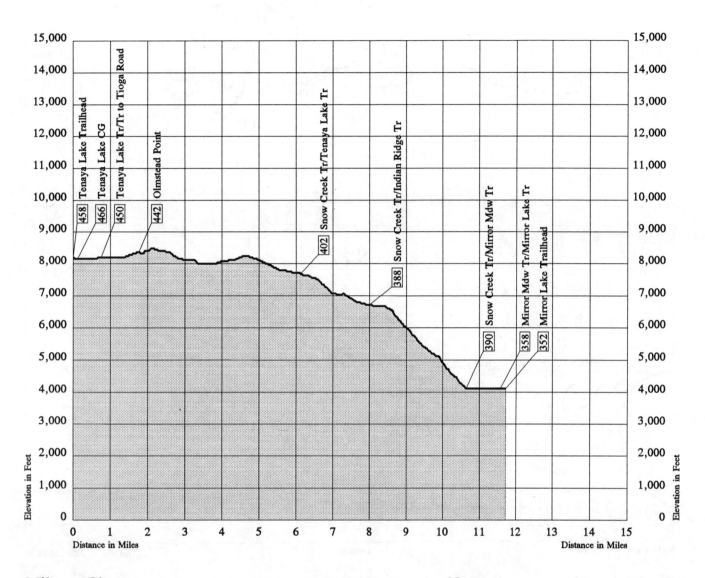

Mileage Chart

Mile	Elevation	Cumulative Distances			Incremental Distances		
		Up	Down	Rating	Up	Down	Rating
0	8,200	0	0	0	0	0	0
1	8,200	40	40	80	40	40	80
2	8,400	280	80	360	240	40	280
3	8,120	360	440	800	80	360	440
4	8,080	440	560	1,000	80	120	200
5	8,120	600	680	1,280	160	120	280
6	7,720	600	1,080	1,680	0	400	400
7	7,080	600	1,720	2,320	0	640	640
8	6,720	640	2,120	2,760	40	400	440
9	6,000	640	2,840	3,480	0	720	720
10	4,920	640	3,920	4,560	0	1,080	1,080
11	4,120	640	4,720	5,360	0	800	800
11.7	4,120	640	4,720	5,360	0	0	0
11.7	Totals	640	4,720	5,360	640	4,720	5,360

Notes

Route:
458 to 402: Tenaya Lake Trail
402 to 390: Snow Creek Trail
390 to 352: Mirror Meadow Trail

See 5C for opposite direction

Map Location

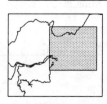

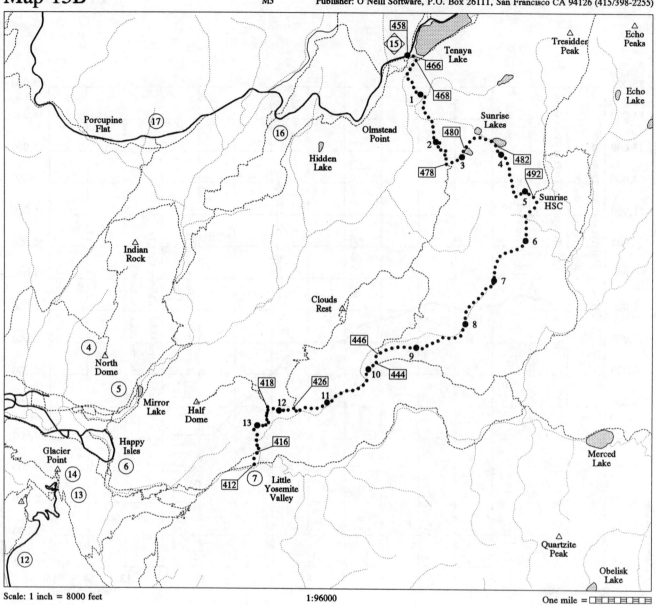

Scale: 1 inch = 8000 feet   1:96000   One mile =

Destination Chart

			Cumulative Distances				Incremental Distances			
Num	Location	Elevation	Miles	Up	Down	Total	Miles	Up	Down	Total
458	Tenaya Lake Trailhead	8,200	0.0	0	0	0	0.0	0	0	0
466	Tenaya Lake CG	8,160	0.1	0	40	40	0.1	0	40	40
468	Forsyth Tr/Tenaya Lake Tr	8,160	0.2	0	40	40	0.1	0	0	0
478	Forsyth Tr/Sunrise Lakes Tr	9,200	2.7	1,040	40	1,080	2.5	1,040	0	1,040
480	Sunrise Lake	9,200	3.2	1,080	80	1,160	0.5	40	40	80
482	Sunrise Lake	9,440	3.8	1,320	80	1,400	0.6	240	0	240
492	Sunrise Lake Tr/John Muir Tr	9,320	5.2	1,640	520	2,160	1.4	320	440	760
446	John Muir Tr/Sunrise Creek Tr	8,000	9.7	2,000	2,200	4,200	4.5	360	1,680	2,040
444	John Muir Tr/High Tr	7,880	9.8	2,000	2,320	4,320	0.1	0	120	120
426	Clouds Rest Tr/John Muir Tr	7,200	11.7	2,040	3,040	5,080	1.9	40	720	760
418	Half Dome Tr/John Muir Tr	7,000	12.2	2,040	3,240	5,280	0.5	0	200	200
416	John Muir Tr/LYV Bypass	6,120	13.6	2,040	4,120	6,160	1.4	0	880	880
412	Little Yosemite Valley	6,120	13.8	2,040	4,120	6,160	0.2	0	0	0
	Totals		13.8	2,040	4,120	6,160	13.8	2,040	4,120	6,160

Tenaya Lake Trailhead to Little Yosemite Valley   15B

Publisher: O'Neill Software, P.O. Box 26111, San Francisco CA 94126 (415/398-2255)

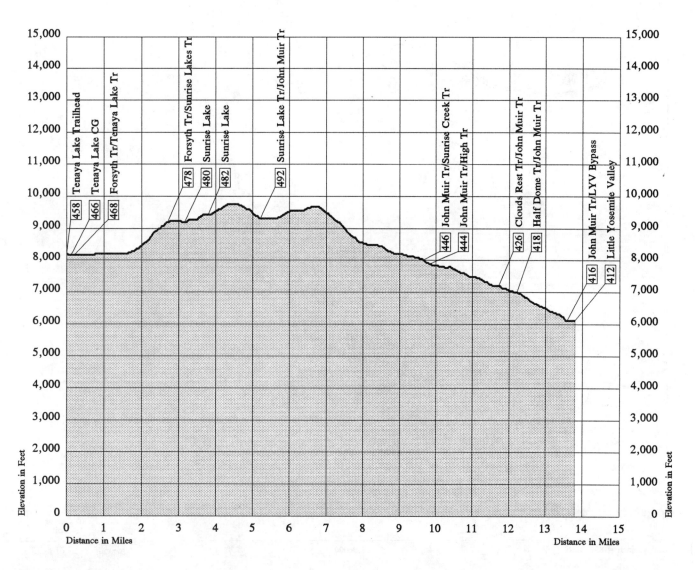

Mileage Chart

		Cumulative Distances			Incremental Distances		
Mile	Elevation	Up	Down	Rating	Up	Down	Rating
0	8,200	0	0	0	0	0	0
1	8,200	40	40	80	40	40	80
2	8,440	280	40	320	240	0	240
3	9,240	1,080	40	1,120	800	0	800
4	9,560	1,440	80	1,520	360	40	400
5	9,480	1,640	360	2,000	200	280	480
6	9,560	1,880	520	2,400	240	160	400
7	9,480	2,000	720	2,720	120	200	320
8	8,520	2,000	1,680	3,680	0	960	960
9	8,200	2,000	2,000	4,000	0	320	320
10	7,840	2,000	2,360	4,360	0	360	360
11	7,480	2,040	2,760	4,800	40	400	440
12	7,040	2,040	3,200	5,240	0	440	440
13	6,480	2,040	3,760	5,800	0	560	560
13.8	6,120	2,040	4,120	6,160	0	360	360
13.8	Totals	2,040	4,120	6,160	2,040	4,120	6,160

Notes

Route:

458 to 468:	Tenaya Lake Trail
468 to 478:	Forsyth Trail
478 to 492:	Sunrise Lakes Trail
492 to 412:	John Muir Trail

See 7B for opposite direction

Map Location

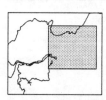

15B   Tenaya Lake Trailhead to Little Yosemite Valley

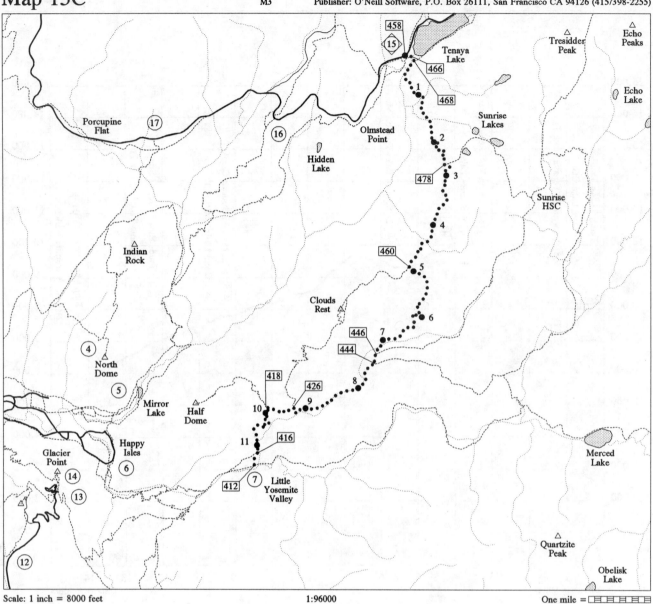

Scale: 1 inch = 8000 feet   1:96000   One mile = ▭▭▭▭▭▭

Destination Chart

Num	Location	Elevation	Cumulative Distances				Incremental Distances			
			Miles	Up	Down	Total	Miles	Up	Down	Total
458	Tenaya Lake Trailhead	8,200	0.0	0	0	0	0.0	0	0	0
466	Tenaya Lake CG	8,160	0.1	0	40	40	0.1	0	40	40
468	Forsyth Tr/Tenaya Lake Tr	8,160	0.2	0	40	40	0.1	0	0	0
478	Forsyth Tr/Sunrise Lakes Tr	9,200	2.7	1,040	40	1,080	2.5	1,040	0	1,040
460	Forsyth Tr/Clouds Rest Tr	9,120	4.9	1,360	440	1,800	2.2	320	400	720
446	John Muir Tr/Sunrise Creek Tr	8,000	7.3	1,360	1,560	2,920	2.4	0	1,120	1,120
444	John Muir Tr/High Tr	7,880	7.4	1,360	1,680	3,040	0.1	0	120	120
426	Clouds Rest Tr/John Muir Tr	7,200	9.3	1,400	2,400	3,800	1.9	40	720	760
418	Half Dome Tr/John Muir Tr	7,000	9.8	1,400	2,600	4,000	0.5	0	200	200
416	John Muir Tr/LYV Bypass	6,120	11.2	1,400	3,480	4,880	1.4	0	880	880
412	Little Yosemite Valley	6,120	11.4	1,400	3,480	4,880	0.2	0	0	0
		Totals	11.4	1,400	3,480	4,880	11.4	1,400	3,480	4,880

Tenaya Lake Trailhead to Little Yosemite Valley   15C

Publisher: O'Neill Software, P.O. Box 26111, San Francisco CA 94126 (415/398-2255)

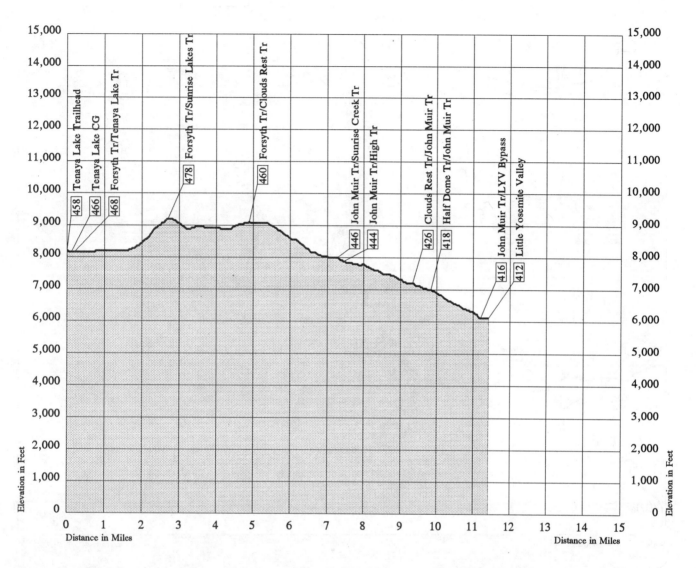

Mileage Chart

Mile	Elevation	Cumulative Distances			Incremental Distances		
		Up	Down	Rating	Up	Down	Rating
0	8,200	0	0	0	0	0	0
1	8,200	40	40	80	40	40	80
2	8,440	280	40	320	240	0	240
3	9,080	1,040	160	1,200	760	120	880
4	8,920	1,120	400	1,520	80	240	320
5	9,080	1,360	480	1,840	240	80	320
6	8,600	1,360	960	2,320	0	480	480
7	8,000	1,360	1,560	2,920	0	600	600
8	7,800	1,400	1,800	3,200	40	240	280
9	7,320	1,400	2,280	3,680	0	480	480
10	6,880	1,400	2,720	4,120	0	440	440
11	6,280	1,400	3,320	4,720	0	600	600
11.4	6,120	1,400	3,480	4,880	0	160	160
11.4	Totals	1,400	3,480	4,880	1,400	3,480	4,880

Notes

Route:

458 to 468:	Tenaya Lake Trail
468 to 446:	Forsyth Trail
446 to 412:	John Muir Trail

See 7C for opposite direction

Map Location

Tenaya Lake Trailhead to Little Yosemite Valley

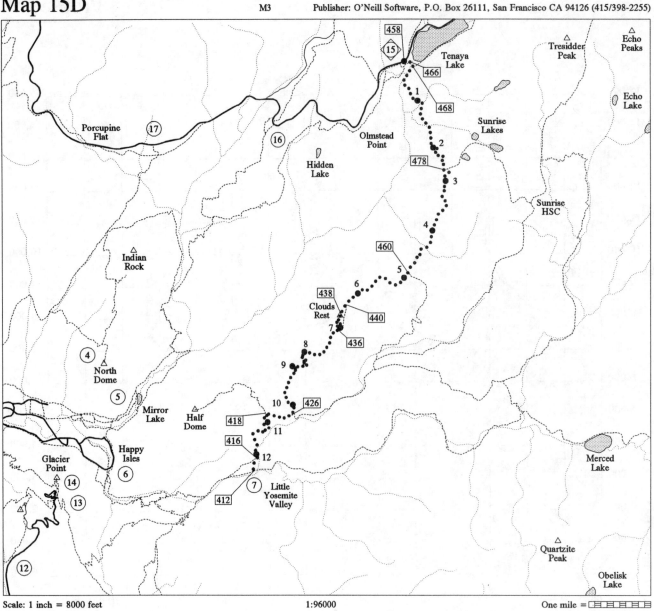

Scale: 1 inch = 8000 feet   1:96000   One mile =

Destination Chart

Num	Location	Elevation	Cumulative Distances				Incremental Distances			
			Miles	Up	Down	Total	Miles	Up	Down	Total
458	Tenaya Lake Trailhead	8,200	0.0	0	0	0	0.0	0	0	0
466	Tenaya Lake CG	8,160	0.1	0	40	40	0.1	0	40	40
468	Forsyth Tr/Tenaya Lake Tr	8,160	0.2	0	40	40	0.1	0	0	0
478	Forsyth Tr/Sunrise Lakes Tr	9,200	2.7	1,040	40	1,080	2.5	1,040	0	1,040
460	Forsyth Tr/Clouds Rest Tr	9,120	4.9	1,360	440	1,800	2.2	320	400	720
440	Clouds Rest Bypass/Clouds Rest Tr	9,760	6.3	2,080	520	2,600	1.4	720	80	800
438	Clouds Rest	9,926	6.4	2,246	520	2,766	0.1	166	0	166
436	Clouds Rest Bypass/Clouds Rest Tr	9,360	7.1	2,246	1,086	3,332	0.7	0	566	566
426	Clouds Rest Tr/John Muir Tr	7,200	10.3	2,246	3,246	5,492	3.2	0	2,160	2,160
418	Half Dome Tr/John Muir Tr	7,000	10.8	2,246	3,446	5,692	0.5	0	200	200
416	John Muir Tr/LYV Bypass	6,120	12.1	2,246	4,326	6,572	1.3	0	880	880
412	Little Yosemite Valley	6,120	12.3	2,246	4,326	6,572	0.2	0	0	0
	Totals		12.3	2,246	4,326	6,572	12.3	2,246	4,326	6,572

Tenaya Lake Trailhead to Little Yosemite Valley   15D

Publisher: O'Neill Software, P.O. Box 26111, San Francisco CA 94126 (415/398-2255)

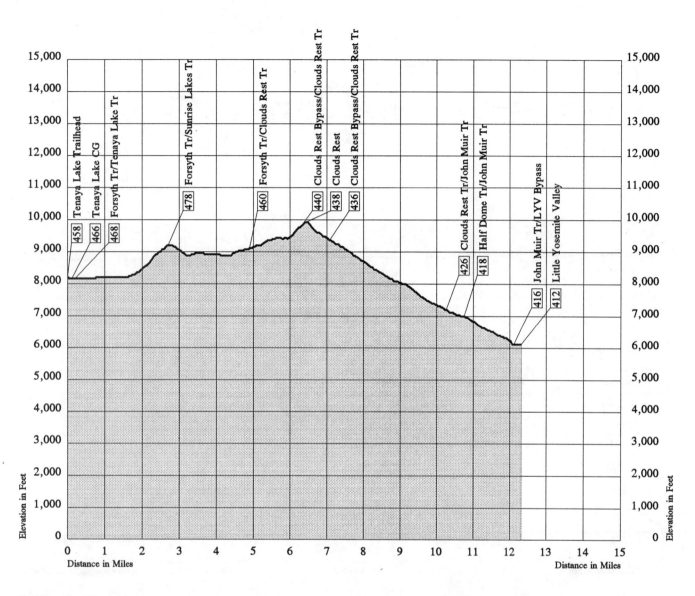

Mileage Chart

Mile	Elevation	Cumulative Distances			Incremental Distances		
		Up	Down	Rating	Up	Down	Rating
0	8,200	0	0	0	0	0	0
1	8,200	40	40	80	40	40	80
2	8,440	280	40	320	240	0	240
3	9,080	1,040	160	1,200	760	120	880
4	8,920	1,120	400	1,520	80	240	320
5	9,160	1,400	440	1,840	280	40	320
6	9,480	1,800	520	2,320	400	80	480
7	9,440	2,246	1,006	3,252	446	486	932
8	8,680	2,246	1,766	4,012	0	760	760
9	8,040	2,246	2,406	4,652	0	640	640
10	7,360	2,246	3,086	5,332	0	680	680
11	6,840	2,246	3,606	5,852	0	520	520
12	6,240	2,246	4,206	6,452	0	600	600
12.3	6,120	2,246	4,326	6,572	0	120	120
12.3	Totals	2,246	4,326	6,572	2,246	4,326	6,572

Notes

Route:
- 458 to 468: Tenaya Lake Trail
- 468 to 460: Forsyth Trail
- 460 to 426: Clouds Rest Trail
- 426 to 412: John Muir Trail

Trail from 440 to 438 not measured

Map Location

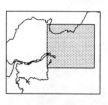

M3   Publisher: O'Neill Software, P.O. Box 26111, San Francisco CA 94126 (415/398-2255)

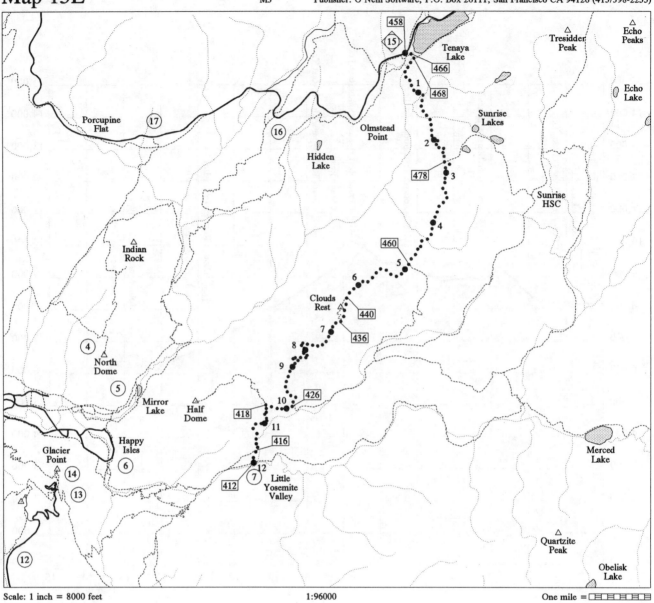

Scale: 1 inch = 8000 feet   1:96000   One mile =

Destination Chart

Num	Location	Elevation	Cumulative Distances				Incremental Distances			
			Miles	Up	Down	Total	Miles	Up	Down	Total
458	Tenaya Lake Trailhead	8,200	0.0	0	0	0	0.0	0	0	0
466	Tenaya Lake CG	8,160	0.1	0	40	40	0.1	0	40	40
468	Forsyth Tr/Tenaya Lake Tr	8,160	0.2	0	40	40	0.1	0	0	0
478	Forsyth Tr/Sunrise Lakes Tr	9,200	2.7	1,040	40	1,080	2.5	1,040	0	1,040
460	Forsyth Tr/Clouds Rest Tr	9,120	4.9	1,360	440	1,800	2.2	320	400	720
440	Clouds Rest Bypass/Clouds Rest Tr	9,760	6.3	2,080	520	2,600	1.4	720	80	800
436	Clouds Rest Bypass/Clouds Rest Tr	9,360	6.7	2,080	920	3,000	0.4	0	400	400
426	Clouds Rest Tr/John Muir Tr	7,200	9.9	2,080	3,080	5,160	3.2	0	2,160	2,160
418	Half Dome Tr/John Muir Tr	7,000	10.4	2,080	3,280	5,360	0.5	0	200	200
416	John Muir Tr/LYV Bypass	6,120	11.8	2,080	4,160	6,240	1.4	0	880	880
412	Little Yosemite Valley	6,120	12.0	2,080	4,160	6,240	0.2	0	0	0
		Totals	12.0	2,080	4,160	6,240	12.0	2,080	4,160	6,240

Tenaya Lake Trailhead to Little Yosemite Valley   15E

Publisher: O'Neill Software, P.O. Box 26111, San Francisco CA 94126 (415/398-2255)

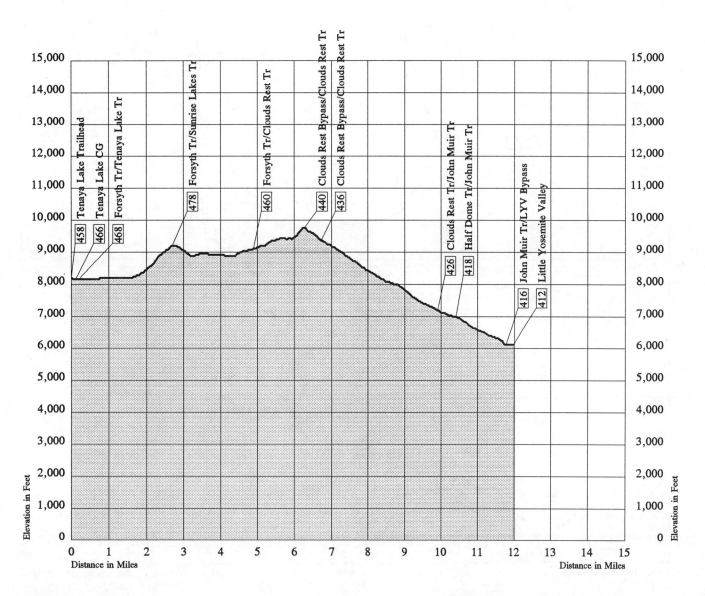

Mileage Chart

Mile	Elevation	Cumulative Distances			Incremental Distances		
		Up	Down	Rating	Up	Down	Rating
0	8,200	0	0	0	0	0	0
1	8,200	40	40	80	40	40	80
2	8,440	280	40	320	240	0	240
3	9,080	1,040	160	1,200	760	120	880
4	8,920	1,120	400	1,520	80	240	320
5	9,160	1,400	440	1,840	280	40	320
6	9,480	1,800	520	2,320	400	80	480
7	9,160	2,080	1,120	3,200	280	600	880
8	8,440	2,080	1,840	3,920	0	720	720
9	7,840	2,080	2,440	4,520	0	600	600
10	7,120	2,080	3,160	5,240	0	720	720
11	6,600	2,080	3,680	5,760	0	520	520
12.0	6,120	2,080	4,160	6,240	0	480	480
12.0	Totals	2,080	4,160	6,240	2,080	4,160	6,240

Notes

Route:

458 to 468:	Tenaya Lake Trail
468 to 460:	Forsyth Trail
460 to 440:	Clouds Rest Trail
440 to 436:	Clouds Rest Bypass
436 to 426:	Clouds Rest Trail
426 to 412:	John Muir Trail

Map Location

M2   Publisher: O'Neill Software, P.O. Box 26111, San Francisco CA 94126 (415/398-2255)

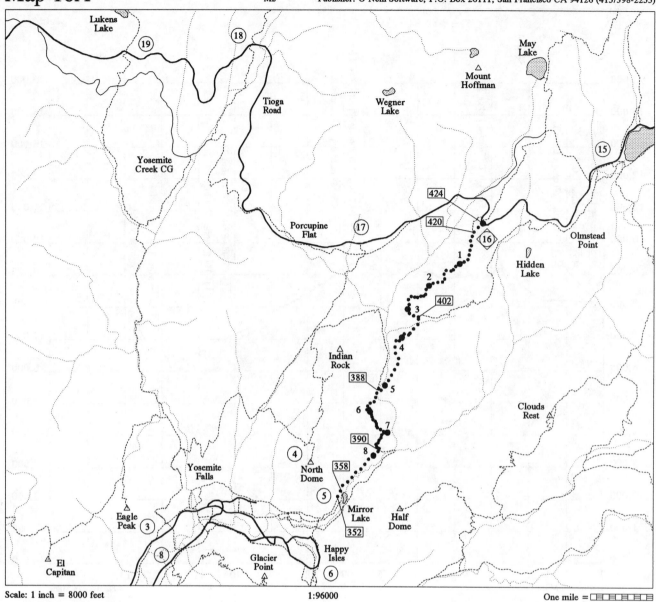

Scale: 1 inch = 8000 feet   1:96000   One mile =

Destination Chart

Num	Location	Elevation	Cumulative Distances				Incremental Distances			
			Miles	Up	Down	Total	Miles	Up	Down	Total
424	Snow Creek Trailhead	8,560	0.0	0	0	0	0.0	0	0	0
420	Snow Creek Tr/Quarry Tr	8,600	0.2	40	0	40	0.2	40	0	40
402	Snow Creek Tr/Tenaya Lake Tr	7,680	3.3	40	920	960	3.1	0	920	920
388	Snow Creek Tr/Indian Ridge Tr	6,720	5.2	80	1,920	2,000	1.9	40	1,000	1,040
390	Snow Creek Tr/Mirror Mdw Tr	4,120	7.9	80	4,520	4,600	2.7	0	2,600	2,600
358	Mirror Mdw Tr/Mirror Lake Tr	4,120	8.8	80	4,520	4,600	0.9	0	0	0
352	Mirror Lake Trailhead	4,120	8.9	80	4,520	4,600	0.1	0	0	0
	Totals		8.9	80	4,520	4,600	8.9	80	4,520	4,600

Snow Creek Trailhead to Mirror Lake Trailhead   16A

Publisher: O'Neill Software, P.O. Box 26111, San Francisco CA 94126 (415/398-2255)

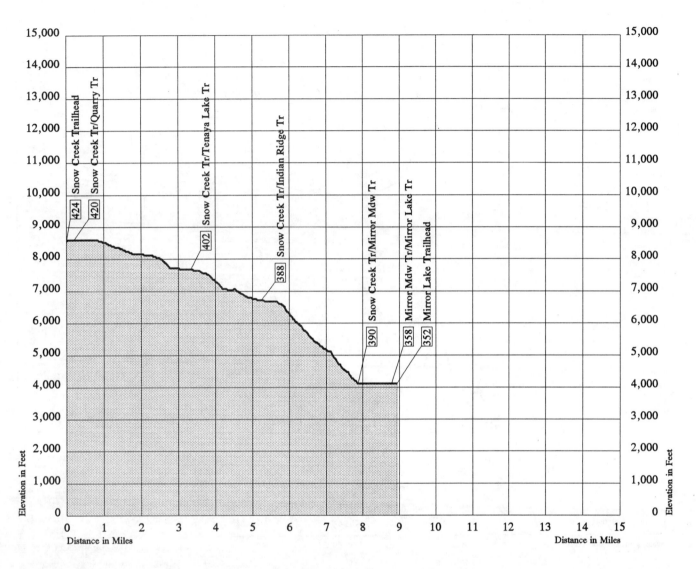

Mileage Chart

		Cumulative Distances			Incremental Distances		
Mile	Elevation	Up	Down	Rating	Up	Down	Rating
0	8,560	0	0	0	0	0	0
1	8,520	40	80	120	40	80	120
2	8,160	40	440	480	0	360	360
3	7,720	40	880	920	0	440	440
4	7,280	40	1,320	1,360	0	440	440
5	6,760	80	1,880	1,960	40	560	600
6	6,280	80	2,360	2,440	0	480	480
7	5,160	80	3,480	3,560	0	1,120	1,120
8	4,120	80	4,520	4,600	0	1,040	1,040
8.9	4,120	80	4,520	4,600	0	0	0
8.9	Totals	80	4,520	4,600	80	4,520	4,600

Notes

Route:

424 to 390:	Snow Creek Trail
390 to 352:	Mirror Meadow Trail

See 5B for opposite direction

Map Location

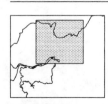

Snow Creek Trailhead to Mirror Lake Trailhead

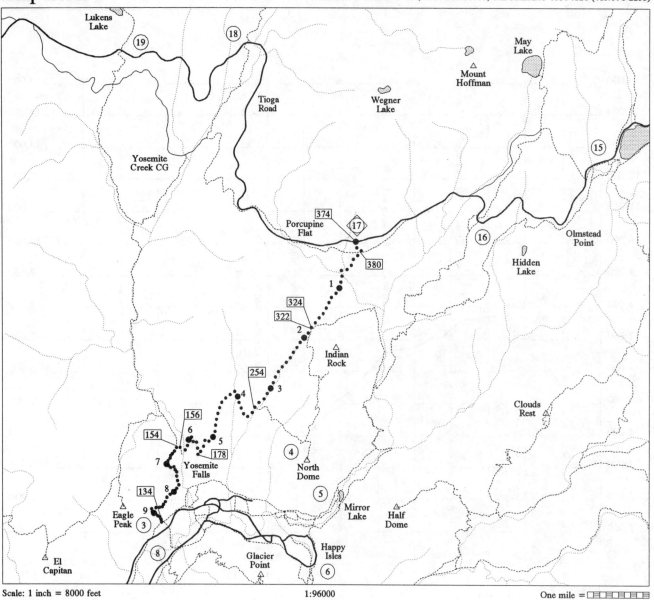

Scale: 1 inch = 8000 feet   1:96000   One mile =

Destination Chart

Num	Location	Elevation	Cumulative Distances				Incremental Distances			
			Miles	Up	Down	Total	Miles	Up	Down	Total
374	Porcupine Creek Trailhead	8,120	0.0	0	0	0	0.0	0	0	0
380	Porcupine Creek Tr/Old Tioga Rd	7,960	0.2	0	160	160	0.2	0	160	160
324	Indian Ridge Tr/Porcupine Creek Tr	7,840	1.8	40	320	360	1.6	40	160	200
322	Indian Ridge Tr/Lehamite Tr	7,840	1.8	40	320	360	0.0	0	0	0
254	North Dome Tr/Lehamite Tr	7,000	3.4	40	1,160	1,200	1.6	0	840	840
178	Yosemite Point	7,000	5.5	480	1,600	2,080	2.1	440	440	880
156	North Dome Tr/Tr to Yosemite Falls	6,680	6.3	560	2,000	2,560	0.8	80	400	480
154	Yosemite Falls Tr/North Dome Tr	6,640	6.4	560	2,040	2,600	0.1	0	40	40
134	Yosemite Falls Trailhead	4,000	9.5	760	4,880	5,640	3.1	200	2,840	3,040
	Totals		9.5	760	4,880	5,640	9.5	760	4,880	5,640

Porcupine Creek Trailhead to Yosemite Falls Trailhead   17A

Publisher: O'Neill Software, P.O. Box 26111, San Francisco CA 94126 (415/398-2255)

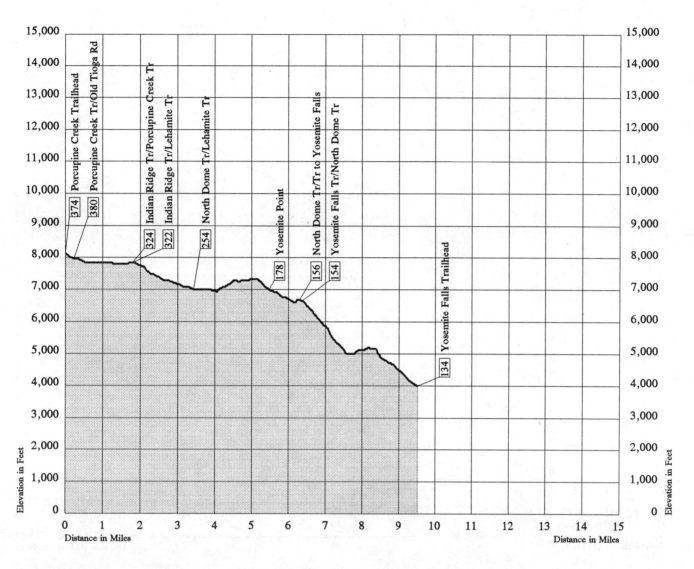

Mileage Chart

Mile	Elevation	Cumulative Distances			Incremental Distances		
		Up	Down	Rating	Up	Down	Rating
0	8,120	0	0	0	0	0	0
1	7,840	0	280	280	0	280	280
2	7,760	40	400	440	40	120	160
3	7,160	40	1,000	1,040	0	600	600
4	6,960	40	1,200	1,240	0	200	200
5	7,320	480	1,280	1,760	440	80	520
6	6,680	480	1,920	2,400	0	640	640
7	5,880	560	2,800	3,360	80	880	960
8	5,120	680	3,680	4,360	120	880	1,000
9	4,480	760	4,400	5,160	80	720	800
9.5	4,000	760	4,880	5,640	0	480	480
9.5	Totals	760	4,880	5,640	760	4,880	5,640

Notes

Route:

374 to 322:	Porcupine Creek Trail
322 to 254:	Lehamite Trail
254 to 154:	North Dome Trail
154 to 134:	Yosemite Falls Trail

Trail from 322 to 254 not measured
See 3C for opposite direction

Map Location

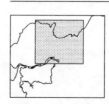

Porcupine Creek Trailhead to Yosemite Falls Trailhead

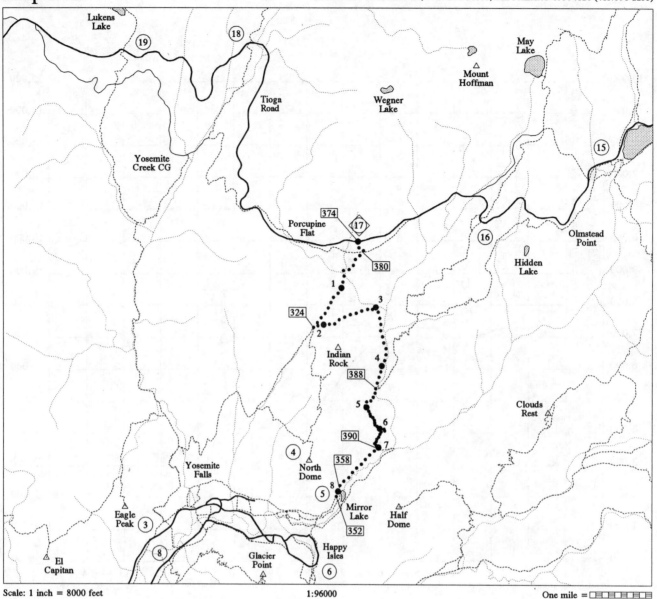

Scale: 1 inch = 8000 feet   1:96000   One mile = ▯▯▯▯▯▯

Destination Chart

Num	Location	Elevation	Cumulative Distances				Incremental Distances			
			Miles	Up	Down	Total	Miles	Up	Down	Total
374	Porcupine Creek Trailhead	8,120	0.0	0	0	0	0.0	0	0	0
380	Porcupine Creek Tr/Old Tioga Rd	7,960	0.2	0	160	160	0.2	0	160	160
324	Indian Ridge Tr/Porcupine Creek Tr	7,840	1.8	40	320	360	1.6	40	160	200
388	Snow Creek Tr/Indian Ridge Tr	6,720	4.4	40	1,440	1,480	2.6	0	1,120	1,120
390	Snow Creek Tr/Mirror Mdw Tr	4,120	7.0	40	4,040	4,080	2.6	0	2,600	2,600
358	Mirror Mdw Tr/Mirror Lake Tr	4,120	7.9	40	4,040	4,080	0.9	0	0	0
352	Mirror Lake Trailhead	4,120	8.1	40	4,040	4,080	0.2	0	0	0
		Totals	8.1	40	4,040	4,080	8.1	40	4,040	4,080

Porcupine Creek Trailhead to Mirror Lake Trailhead   17B

Publisher: O'Neill Software, P.O. Box 26111, San Francisco CA 94126 (415/398-2255)

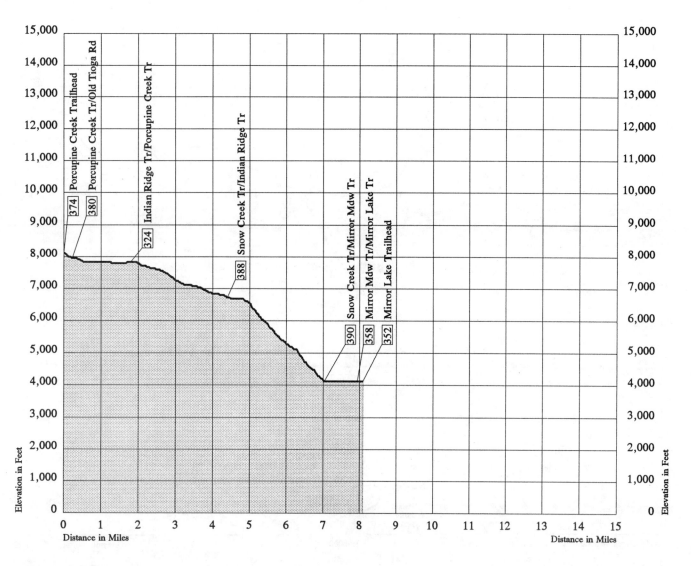

Mileage Chart

		Cumulative Distances			Incremental Distances		
Mile	Elevation	Up	Down	Rating	Up	Down	Rating
0	8,120	0	0	0	0	0	0
1	7,840	0	280	280	0	280	280
2	7,800	40	360	400	40	80	120
3	7,280	40	880	920	0	520	520
4	6,840	40	1,320	1,360	0	440	440
5	6,520	40	1,640	1,680	0	320	320
6	5,280	40	2,880	2,920	0	1,240	1,240
7	4,160	40	4,000	4,040	0	1,120	1,120
8	4,120	40	4,040	4,080	0	40	40
8.1	4,120	40	4,040	4,080	0	0	0
8.1	Totals	40	4,040	4,080	40	4,040	4,080

Notes

Route:

374 to 324:	Porcupine Creek Trail
324 to 388:	Indian Ridge Trail
388 to 390:	Snow Creek Trail
390 to 352:	Mirror Meadow Trail

See 5A for opposite direction

Map Location

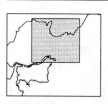

Porcupine Creek Trailhead to Mirror Lake Trailhead

M2   Publisher: O'Neill Software, P.O. Box 26111, San Francisco CA 94126 (415/398-2255)

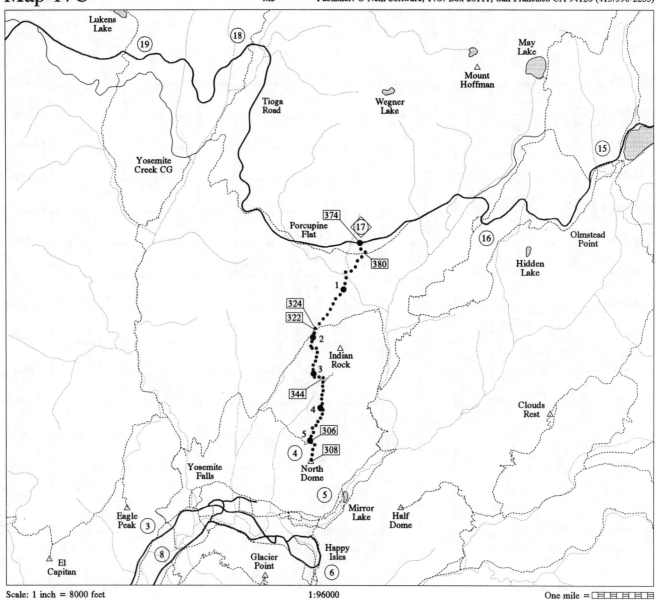

Scale: 1 inch = 8000 feet   1:96000   One mile =

Destination Chart

Num	Location	Elevation	Cumulative Distances				Incremental Distances			
			Miles	Up	Down	Total	Miles	Up	Down	Total
374	Porcupine Creek Trailhead	8,120	0.0	0	0	0	0.0	0	0	0
380	Porcupine Creek Tr/Old Tioga Rd	7,960	0.2	0	160	160	0.2	0	160	160
324	Indian Ridge Tr/Porcupine Creek Tr	7,840	1.8	40	320	360	1.6	40	160	200
322	Indian Ridge Tr/Lehamite Tr	7,840	1.8	40	320	360	0.0	0	0	0
344	Indian Ridge Tr/Natural Arch Tr	8,120	3.3	400	400	800	1.5	360	80	440
306	North Dome Tr/Indian Ridge Tr	7,560	5.0	440	1,000	1,440	1.7	40	600	640
308	North Dome	7,542	5.5	582	1,160	1,742	0.5	142	160	302
	Totals		5.5	582	1,160	1,742	5.5	582	1,160	1,742

Porcupine Creek Trailhead to North Dome

Publisher: O'Neill Software, P.O. Box 26111, San Francisco CA 94126 (415/398-2255)

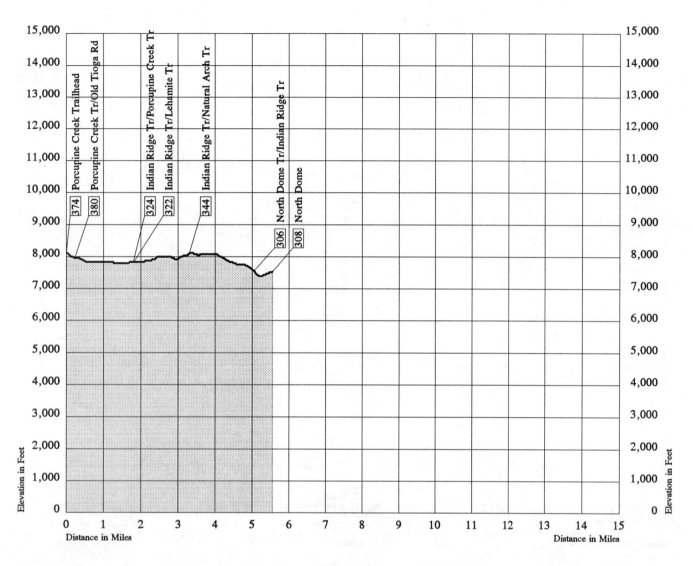

Mileage Chart

		Cumulative Distances			Incremental Distances		
Mile	Elevation	Up	Down	Rating	Up	Down	Rating
0	8,120	0	0	0	0	0	0
1	7,840	0	280	280	0	280	280
2	7,840	40	320	360	40	40	80
3	7,960	240	400	640	200	80	280
4	8,080	440	480	920	200	80	280
5	7,600	440	960	1,400	0	480	480
5.5	7,542	582	1,160	1,742	142	200	342
5.5	Totals	582	1,160	1,742	582	1,160	1,742

Notes

Route:
374 to 322:	Porcupine Creek Trail
322 to 306:	Indian Ridge Trail
306 to 308:	North Dome Trail

Map Location

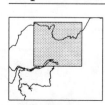

M2   Publisher: O'Neill Software, P.O. Box 26111, San Francisco CA 94126 (415/398-2255)

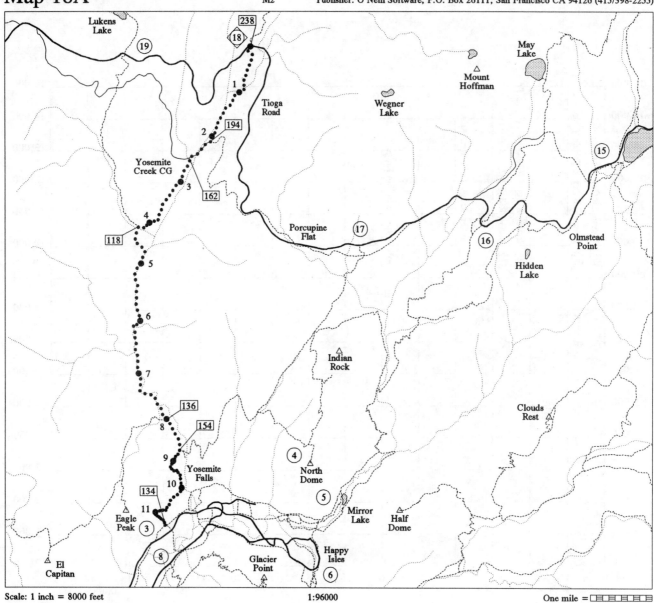

Scale: 1 inch = 8000 feet   1:96000   One mile =

Destination Chart

Num	Location	Elevation	Cumulative Distances				Incremental Distances			
			Miles	Up	Down	Total	Miles	Up	Down	Total
238	Yosemite Creek Trailhead	7,480	0.0	0	0	0	0.0	0	0	0
194	Yosemite Creek Tr/Old Tioga Rd	7,200	2.1	0	280	280	2.1	0	280	280
162	Yosemite Creek Campground	7,160	2.6	0	320	320	0.5	0	40	40
118	Yosemite Creek Tr/Hetch Hetchy Tr	7,160	4.3	160	480	640	1.7	160	160	320
136	El Capitan Tr/Yosemite Creek Tr	6,840	8.0	200	840	1,040	3.7	40	360	400
154	Yosemite Falls Tr/North Dome Tr	6,640	8.6	280	1,120	1,400	0.6	80	280	360
134	Yosemite Falls Trailhead	4,000	11.7	480	3,960	4,440	3.1	200	2,840	3,040
	Totals		11.7	480	3,960	4,440	11.7	480	3,960	4,440

Yosemite Creek Trailhead to Yosemite Falls Trailhead   18A

Publisher: O'Neill Software, P.O. Box 26111, San Francisco CA 94126 (415/398-2255)

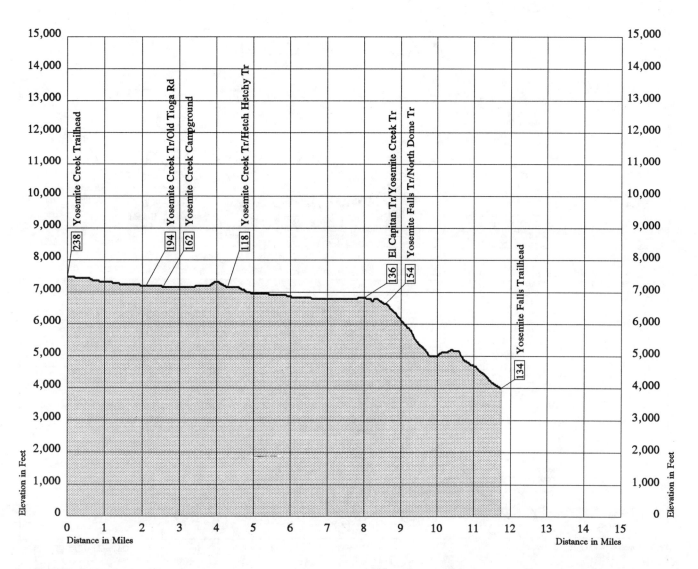

Mileage Chart

Mile	Elevation	Cumulative Distances			Incremental Distances		
		Up	Down	Rating	Up	Down	Rating
0	7,480	0	0	0	0	0	0
1	7,320	0	160	160	0	160	160
2	7,200	0	280	280	0	120	120
3	7,160	0	320	320	0	40	40
4	7,320	160	320	480	160	0	160
5	6,960	160	680	840	0	360	360
6	6,880	160	760	920	0	80	80
7	6,800	160	840	1,000	0	80	80
8	6,840	200	840	1,040	40	0	40
9	6,120	280	1,640	1,920	80	800	880
10	5,000	280	2,760	3,040	0	1,120	1,120
11	4,680	480	3,280	3,760	200	520	720
11.7	4,000	480	3,960	4,440	0	680	680
11.7	Totals	480	3,960	4,440	480	3,960	4,440

Notes

Route:
    238 to 194:   Yosemite Creek Trail
    194 to 162:   Old Tioga Road
    162 to 154:   Yosemite Creek Trail
    154 to 134:   Yosemite Falls Trail

See 3B for opposite direction

Map Location

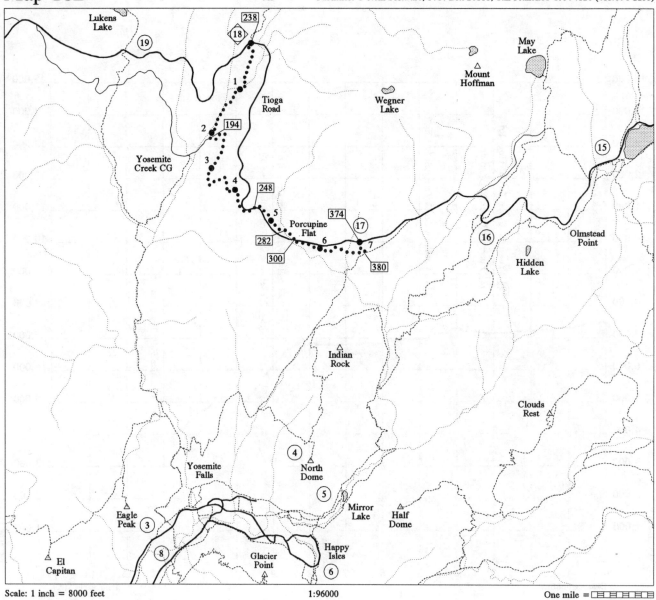

Scale: 1 inch = 8000 feet   1:96000   One mile = ▭▭▭▭▭▭

Destination Chart

Num	Location	Elevation	Cumulative Distances				Incremental Distances			
			Miles	Up	Down	Total	Miles	Up	Down	Total
238	Yosemite Creek Trailhead	7,480	0.0	0	0	0	0.0	0	0	0
194	Yosemite Creek Tr/Old Tioga Rd	7,200	2.1	0	280	280	2.1	0	280	280
248	Tioga Road Crossing	8,280	4.6	1,080	280	1,360	2.5	1,080	0	1,080
282	Porcupine Flat Campground	8,120	5.3	1,080	440	1,520	0.7	0	160	160
300	Porcupine Flat/Tioga Rd	8,120	5.5	1,080	440	1,520	0.2	0	0	0
380	Porcupine Creek Tr/Old Tioga Rd	7,960	6.8	1,080	600	1,680	1.3	0	160	160
374	Porcupine Creek Trailhead	8,120	7.0	1,240	600	1,840	0.2	160	0	160
		Totals	7.0	1,240	600	1,840	7.0	1,240	600	1,840

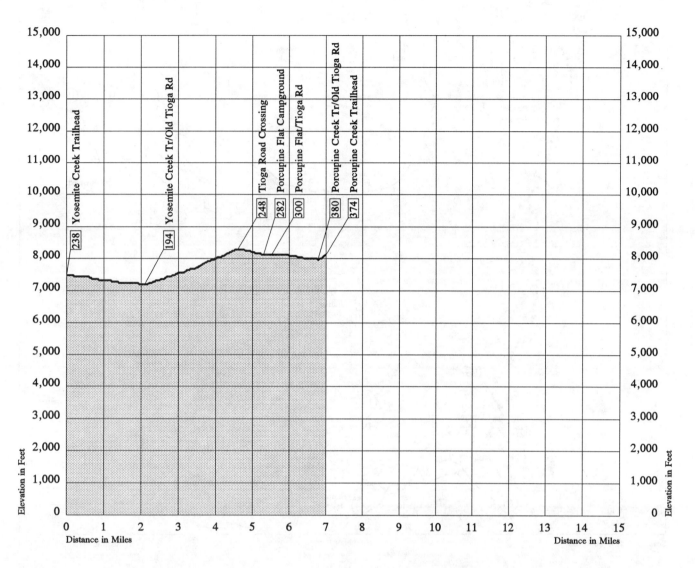

Mileage Chart

		Cumulative Distances			Incremental Distances		
Mile	Elevation	Up	Down	Rating	Up	Down	Rating
0	7,480	0	0	0	0	0	0
1	7,320	0	160	160	0	160	160
2	7,200	0	280	280	0	120	120
3	7,560	360	280	640	360	0	360
4	8,000	800	280	1,080	440	0	440
5	8,200	1,080	360	1,440	280	80	360
6	8,080	1,080	480	1,560	0	120	120
7	8,120	1,240	600	1,840	160	120	280
7.0	Totals	1,240	600	1,840	1,240	600	1,840

Notes

Route:

238 to 194:	Yosemite Creek Trail
194 to 380:	Old Tioga Road
380 to 374:	Porcupine Creek Trail

Trail from 194 to 380 not measured

Map Location

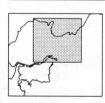

M2   Publisher: O'Neill Software, P.O. Box 26111, San Francisco CA 94126 (415/398-2255)

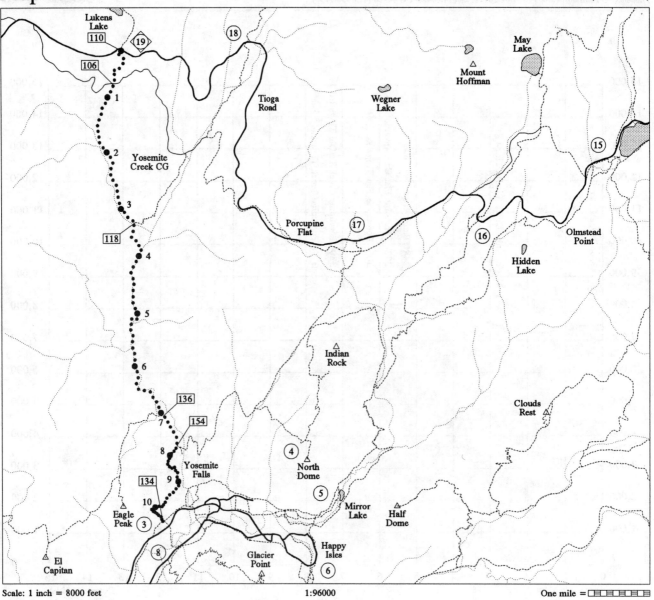

Scale: 1 inch = 8000 feet   1:96000   One mile =

Destination Chart

Num	Location	Elevation	Cumulative Distances				Incremental Distances			
			Miles	Up	Down	Total	Miles	Up	Down	Total
110	Tioga Road	8,160	0.0	0	0	0	0.0	0	0	0
106	Hetch Hetchy Tr/Old Tioga Rd	7,960	0.8	0	200	200	0.8	0	200	200
118	Yosemite Creek Tr/Hetch Hetchy Tr	7,160	3.4	0	1,000	1,000	2.6	0	800	800
136	El Capitan Tr/Yosemite Creek Tr	6,840	7.1	40	1,360	1,400	3.7	40	360	400
154	Yosemite Falls Tr/North Dome Tr	6,640	7.6	120	1,640	1,760	0.5	80	280	360
134	Yosemite Falls Trailhead	4,000	10.8	320	4,480	4,800	3.2	200	2,840	3,040
		Totals	10.8	320	4,480	4,800	10.8	320	4,480	4,800

Tioga Road to Yosemite Falls Trailhead

Publisher: O'Neill Software, P.O. Box 26111, San Francisco CA 94126 (415/398-2255)

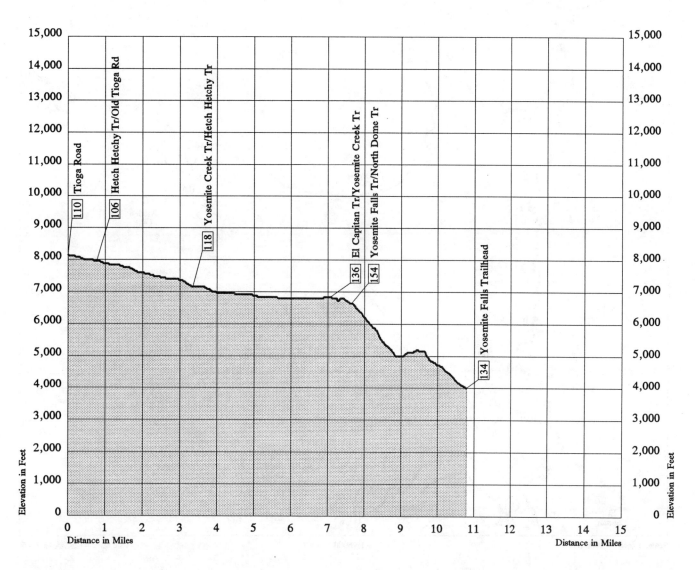

Mileage Chart

		Cumulative Distances			Incremental Distances		
Mile	Elevation	Up	Down	Rating	Up	Down	Rating
0	8,160	0	0	0	0	0	0
1	7,880	0	280	280	0	280	280
2	7,600	0	560	560	0	280	280
3	7,360	0	800	800	0	240	240
4	6,960	0	1,200	1,200	0	400	400
5	6,880	0	1,280	1,280	0	80	80
6	6,800	0	1,360	1,360	0	80	80
7	6,840	40	1,360	1,400	40	0	40
8	6,200	120	2,080	2,200	80	720	800
9	5,000	120	3,280	3,400	0	1,200	1,200
10	4,720	320	3,760	4,080	200	480	680
10.8	4,000	320	4,480	4,800	0	720	720
10.8	Totals	320	4,480	4,800	320	4,480	4,800

Notes

Route:

110 to 118:	Hetch Hetchy Trail
118 to 154:	Yosemite Creek Trail
154 to 134:	Yosemite Falls Trail

Trail from 110 to 106 not measured
See 3A for opposite direction

Map Location

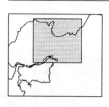

Tioga Road to Yosemite Falls Trailhead

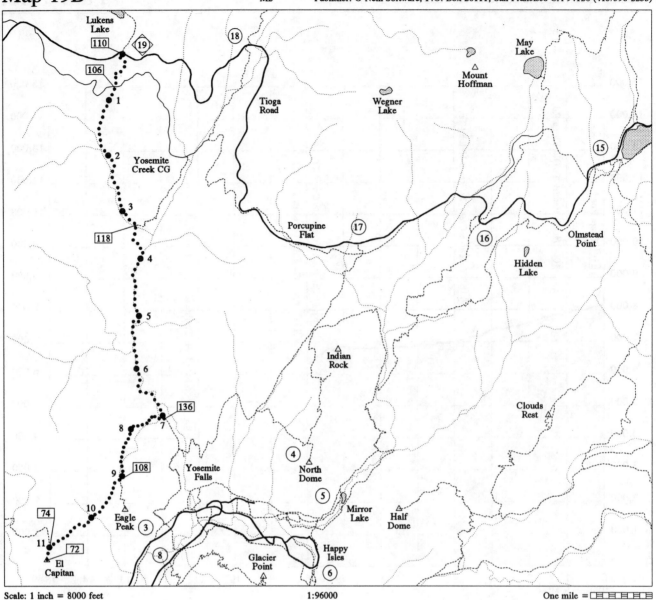

Scale: 1 inch = 8000 feet   1:96000   One mile =

Destination Chart

Num	Location	Elevation	Cumulative Distances				Incremental Distances			
			Miles	Up	Down	Total	Miles	Up	Down	Total
110	Tioga Road	8,160	0.0	0	0	0	0.0	0	0	0
106	Hetch Hetchy Tr/Old Tioga Rd	7,960	0.8	0	200	200	0.8	0	200	200
118	Yosemite Creek Tr/Hetch Hetchy Tr	7,160	3.4	0	1,000	1,000	2.6	0	800	800
136	El Capitan Tr/Yosemite Creek Tr	6,840	7.1	40	1,360	1,400	3.7	40	360	400
108	Eagle Peak Tr/El Capitan Tr	7,360	9.1	560	1,360	1,920	2.0	520	0	520
74	El Capitan Tr/Tr to El Capitan Top	7,600	11.0	1,080	1,640	2,720	1.9	520	280	800
72	El Capitan	7,569	11.2	1,089	1,680	2,769	0.2	9	40	49
		Totals	11.2	1,089	1,680	2,769	11.2	1,089	1,680	2,769

Publisher: O'Neill Software, P.O. Box 26111, San Francisco CA 94126 (415/398-2255)

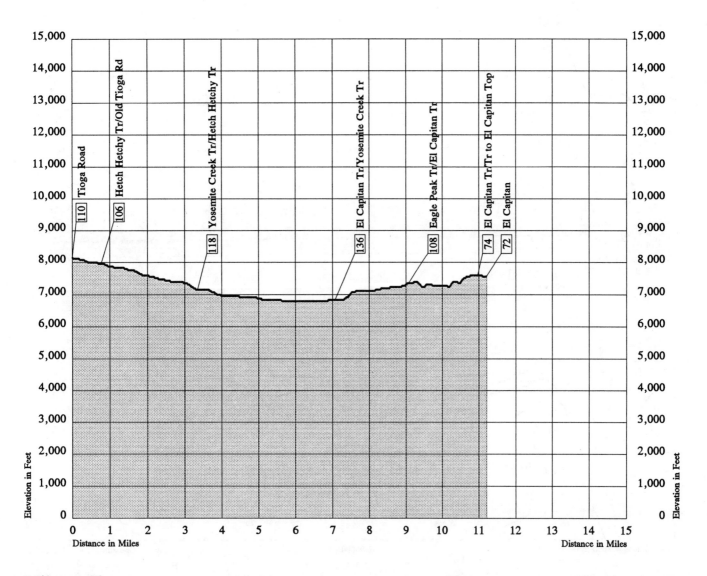

Mileage Chart

Mile	Elevation	Cumulative Distances			Incremental Distances		
		Up	Down	Rating	Up	Down	Rating
0	8,160	0	0	0	0	0	0
1	7,880	0	280	280	0	280	280
2	7,600	0	560	560	0	280	280
3	7,360	0	800	800	0	240	240
4	6,960	0	1,200	1,200	0	400	400
5	6,880	0	1,280	1,280	0	80	80
6	6,800	0	1,360	1,360	0	80	80
7	6,840	40	1,360	1,400	40	0	40
8	7,120	320	1,360	1,680	280	0	280
9	7,320	520	1,360	1,880	200	0	200
10	7,280	680	1,560	2,240	160	200	360
11	7,600	1,080	1,640	2,720	400	80	480
11.2	7,569	1,089	1,680	2,769	9	40	49
11.2	Totals	1,089	1,680	2,769	1,089	1,680	2,769

Notes

Route:

110 to 118:	Hetch Hetchy Trail
118 to 136:	Yosemite Creek Trail
136 to 74:	El Capitan Trail
74 to 72:	Trail to El Capitan Top

Trail from 110 to 106 not measured

Map Location

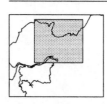

Tioga Road to El Capitan

M1   Publisher: O'Neill Software, P.O. Box 26111, San Francisco CA 94126 (415/398-2255)

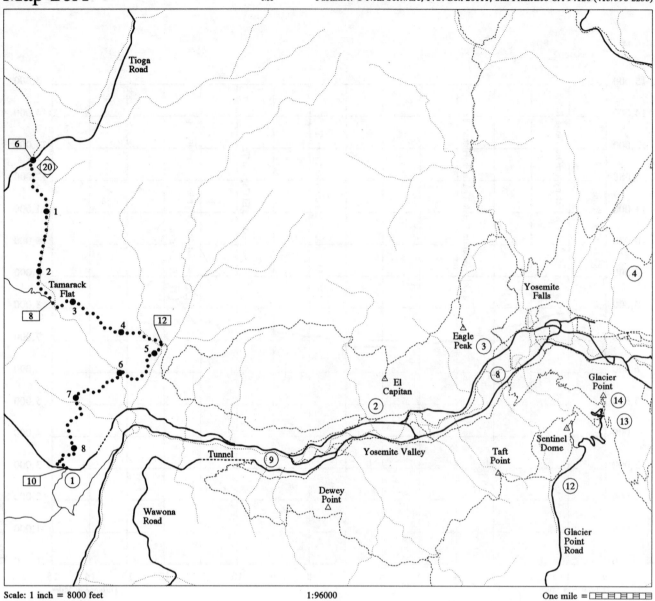

Scale: 1 inch = 8000 feet   1:96000   One mile =

Destination Chart

Num	Location	Elevation	Cumulative Distances				Incremental Distances			
			Miles	Up	Down	Total	Miles	Up	Down	Total
6	Tamarack Creek Trailhead	6,760	0.0	0	0	0	0.0	0	0	0
8	Tamarack Flat Campground	6,320	2.6	0	440	440	2.6	0	440	440
12	Tamarack Creek Tr/Rockslide Rt	6,000	4.8	200	960	1,160	2.2	200	520	720
10	Big Oak Flat Road	4,760	8.8	560	2,560	3,120	4.0	360	1,600	1,960
		Totals	8.8	560	2,560	3,120	8.8	560	2,560	3,120

Tamarack Creek Trailhead to Big Oak Flat Road

Publisher: O'Neill Software, P.O. Box 26111, San Francisco CA 94126 (415/398-2255)

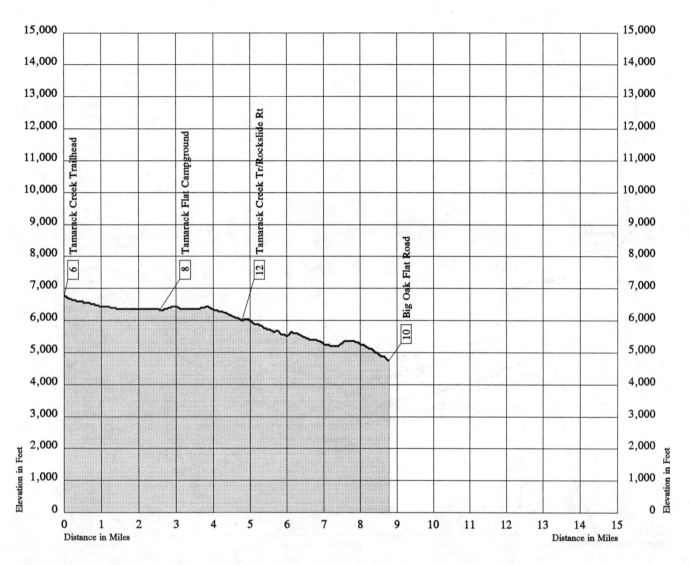

Mileage Chart

Mile	Elevation	Cumulative Distances			Incremental Distances		
		Up	Down	Rating	Up	Down	Rating
0	6,760	0	0	0	0	0	0
1	6,440	0	320	320	0	320	320
2	6,360	0	400	400	0	80	80
3	6,440	120	440	560	120	40	160
4	6,320	200	640	840	80	200	280
5	6,000	240	1,000	1,240	40	360	400
6	5,520	280	1,520	1,800	40	520	560
7	5,240	400	1,920	2,320	120	400	520
8	5,240	560	2,080	2,640	160	160	320
8.8	4,760	560	2,560	3,120	0	480	480
8.8	Totals	560	2,560	3,120	560	2,560	3,120

Notes

Route:
  6 to 10:   Tamarack Creek Trail

Trail from 6 to 12 not measured
See 1A for opposite direction

Map Location

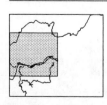

M1   Publisher: O'Neill Software, P.O. Box 26111, San Francisco CA 94126 (415/398-2255)

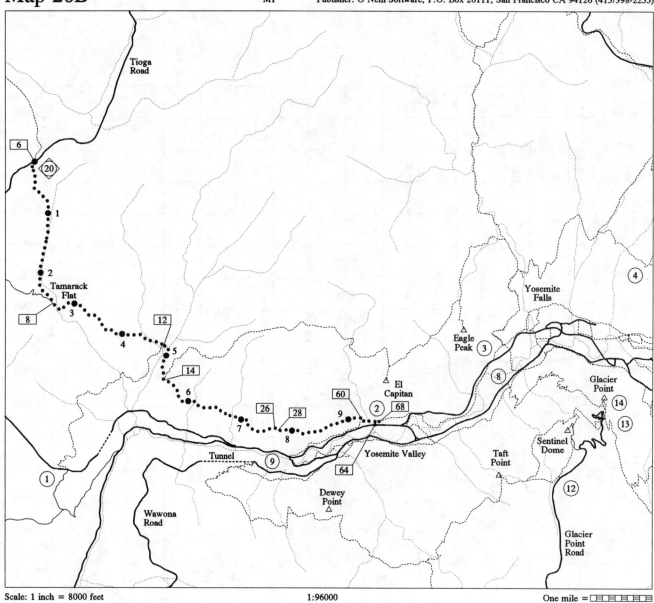

Scale: 1 inch = 8000 feet   1:96000   One mile = ▭▭▭▭▭

Destination Chart

Num	Location	Elevation	Cumulative Distances				Incremental Distances			
			Miles	Up	Down	Total	Miles	Up	Down	Total
6	Tamarack Creek Trailhead	6,760	0.0	0	0	0	0.0	0	0	0
8	Tamarack Flat Campground	6,320	2.6	0	440	440	2.6	0	440	440
12	Tamarack Creek Tr/Rockslide Rt	6,000	4.8	200	960	1,160	2.2	200	520	720
14	El Capitan Tr/Rockslide Rt	5,800	5.4	200	1,160	1,360	0.6	0	200	200
26	Slide Area Top - no trail	4,880	7.7	200	2,080	2,280	2.3	0	920	920
28	Slide Area Bottom - no trail	4,680	7.8	200	2,280	2,480	0.1	0	200	200
60	Rockslide Rt/Valley Tr	4,000	9.3	240	3,000	3,240	1.5	40	720	760
68	Valley Tr	3,960	9.6	240	3,040	3,280	0.3	0	40	40
64	Northside Drive	3,960	9.7	240	3,040	3,280	0.1	0	0	0
	Totals		9.7	240	3,040	3,280	9.7	240	3,040	3,280

Tamarack Creek Trailhead to Northside Drive   20B

Publisher: O'Neill Software, P.O. Box 26111, San Francisco CA 94126 (415/398-2255)

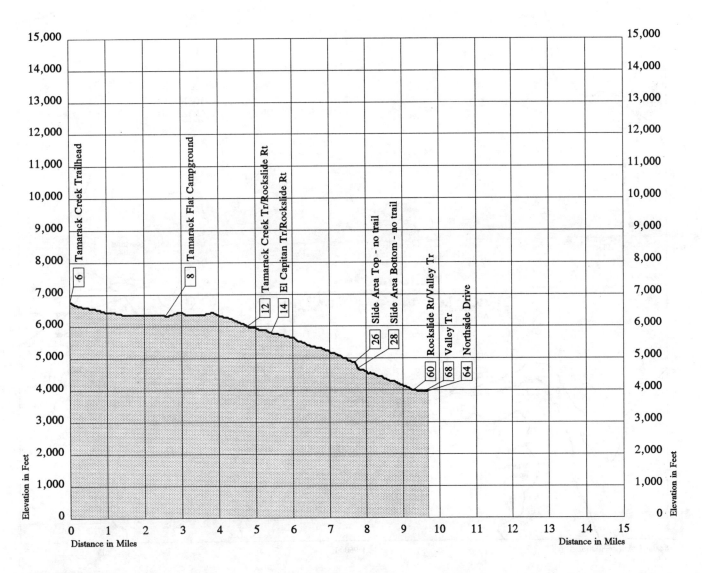

Mileage Chart

Mile	Elevation	Cumulative Distances			Incremental Distances		
		Up	Down	Rating	Up	Down	Rating
0	6,760	0	0	0	0	0	0
1	6,440	0	320	320	0	320	320
2	6,360	0	400	400	0	80	80
3	6,440	120	440	560	120	40	160
4	6,320	200	640	840	80	200	280
5	5,920	200	1,040	1,240	0	400	400
6	5,640	200	1,320	1,520	0	280	280
7	5,160	200	1,800	2,000	0	480	480
8	4,560	200	2,400	2,600	0	600	600
9	4,120	240	2,880	3,120	40	480	520
9.7	3,960	240	3,040	3,280	0	160	160
9.7	Totals	240	3,040	3,280	240	3,040	3,280

Notes

Route:
6 to 12:	Tamarack Creek Trail
12 to 60:	Rockslide Route
60 to 64:	Valley Trail

Trail from 6 to 12 not measured
Trail from 14 to 64 not measured

Map Location

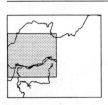

M1   Publisher: O'Neill Software, P.O. Box 26111, San Francisco CA 94126 (415/398-2255)

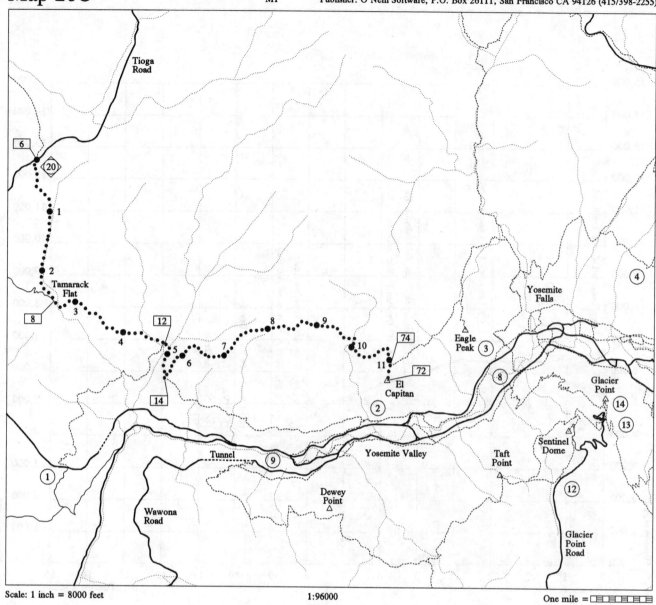

Scale: 1 inch = 8000 feet   1:96000   One mile = ⊞⊞⊞⊞⊞

Destination Chart

Num	Location	Elevation	Cumulative Distances				Incremental Distances			
			Miles	Up	Down	Total	Miles	Up	Down	Total
6	Tamarack Creek Trailhead	6,760	0.0	0	0	0	0.0	0	0	0
8	Tamarack Flat Campground	6,320	2.6	0	440	440	2.6	0	440	440
12	Tamarack Creek Tr/Rockslide Rt	6,000	4.8	200	960	1,160	2.2	200	520	720
14	El Capitan Tr/Rockslide Rt	5,800	5.4	200	1,160	1,360	0.6	0	200	200
74	El Capitan Tr/Tr to El Capitan Top	7,600	11.1	2,400	1,560	3,960	5.7	2,200	400	2,600
72	El Capitan	7,569	11.3	2,409	1,600	4,009	0.2	9	40	49
	Totals		11.3	2,409	1,600	4,009	11.3	2,409	1,600	4,009

Tamarack Creek Trailhead to El Capitan

Publisher: O'Neill Software, P.O. Box 26111, San Francisco CA 94126 (415/398-2255)

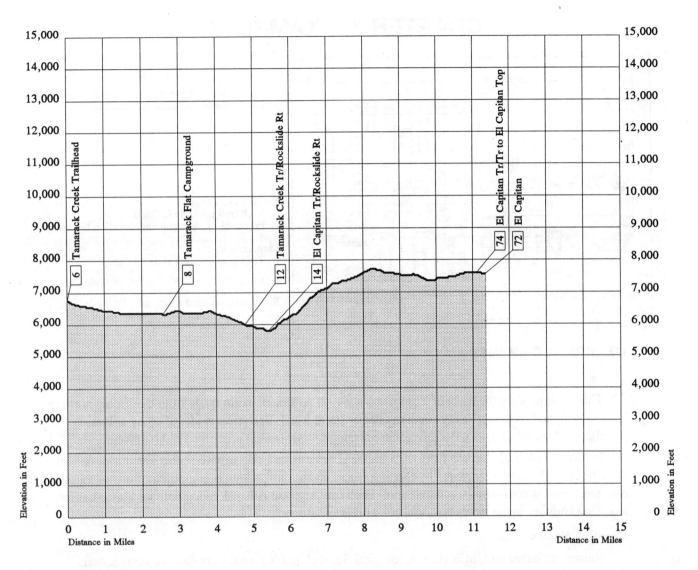

Mileage Chart

Mile	Elevation	Cumulative Distances			Incremental Distances		
		Up	Down	Rating	Up	Down	Rating
0	6,760	0	0	0	0	0	0
1	6,440	0	320	320	0	320	320
2	6,360	0	400	400	0	80	80
3	6,440	120	440	560	120	40	160
4	6,320	200	640	840	80	200	280
5	5,920	200	1,040	1,240	0	400	400
6	6,240	640	1,160	1,800	440	120	560
7	7,120	1,520	1,160	2,680	880	0	880
8	7,600	2,000	1,160	3,160	480	0	480
9	7,560	2,120	1,320	3,440	120	160	280
10	7,400	2,200	1,560	3,760	80	240	320
11	7,600	2,400	1,560	3,960	200	0	200
11.3	7,569	2,409	1,600	4,009	9	40	49
11.3	Totals	2,409	1,600	4,009	2,409	1,600	4,009

Notes

Route:

6 to 12:	Tamarack Creek Trail
12 to 14:	Rockslide Route
14 to 74:	El Capitan Trail
74 to 72:	Trail to El Capitan Top

Trail from 6 to 12 not measured

Map Location

CHAPTER 3: EXAMPLES

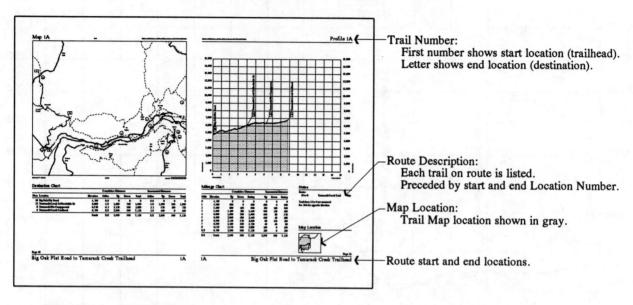

Trail Number:
First number shows start location (trailhead).
Letter shows end location (destination).

Route Description:
Each trail on route is listed.
Preceded by start and end Location Number.

Map Location:
Trail Map location shown in gray.

Route start and end locations.

3.1 GENERAL COMMENTS

Trails

This book profiles the trails of Yosemite Valley. It covers all major trails from the Valley north to Tioga Road, and from the Valley south to Glacier Point Road. Each trail is identified by a Trail Number such as 1A, 1B, etc. Book pages are arranged in sequential order by Trail Number.

In general, all trails leading from each trailhead are profiled. Alternative routes are shown one after the other so they can be compared by flipping pages. Each route, which is composed of one or more trail segments, is considered a separate trail. Each trail segment is listed, along with its Start and End Location Number in the Notes box, under the heading "Route".

Location Names

Names are based on USGS (U.S. Geological Survey) and National Park Service designations. When a trail name is unknown, a name based on its destination or a significant nearby feature is used. Trail junctions are shown as the name of each intersecting trail separated by a slash. For example, Clouds Rest Tr/John Muir Tr. Abbreviations are listed on page 8.

Location Numbers

Features along the trail, such as trail junctions and trailheads, and destinations such as lakes, passes, and peaks are assigned unique Location Numbers so they can be easily identified and cross-referenced. Location Numbers have no meaning outside this book. They are assigned to specific locations on the map, starting at the top left and working down and across the page.

Trail Distances

Distances shown on all maps, profiles and charts in this book are based on actual, measured, on-trail hiking distances obtained from the National Park Service. Exceptions are listed in the Notes, which tell exactly which portion of a trail was not measured.

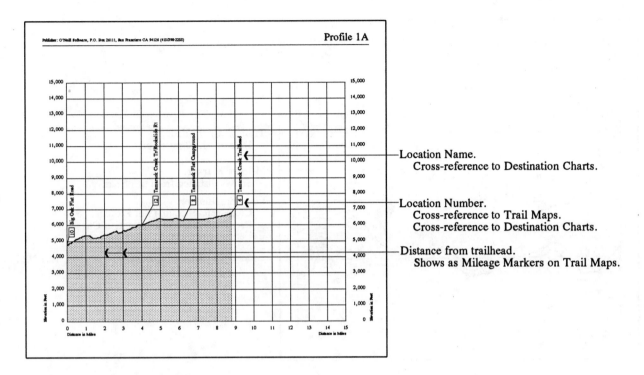

Location Name.
    Cross-reference to Destination Charts.

Location Number.
    Cross-reference to Trail Maps.
    Cross-reference to Destination Charts.

Distance from trailhead.
    Shows as Mileage Markers on Trail Maps.

3.2 READING TRAIL PROFILES

Trail Profile Format

A Trail Profile is like a cross-section through the trail. It tracks the trail along its route, showing true distance and elevation at each point. Although distances and elevations are scaled to exaggerate relationships, they accurately represent the real trail. Trail junctions and other features along the trail are identified and precisely located on each profile, so you can see exactly how they relate to each other.

Trail Profiles plot a trail's elevation with respect to its distance from the trailhead. Distance is shown horizontally, in miles, at a scale of 1 inch = 13,400 feet. Elevation is shown vertically, in feet, at a scale of 1 inch = 3,000 feet. Elevation is therefore exaggerated by almost 4.5 times. The exaggeration is intentional, so elevation changes can be detected more readily.

Distances shown are actual, measured, on-trail distances. Elevation changes are recorded at 40 foot intervals, similar to 7.5 minute topographic maps. This means that a trail shown as perfectly level may in fact undulate as much as 39 feet up or down.

Trail junctions and other major trail features are indicated by their Location Number, shown in a box, followed by Location Name. A line drawn from the box shows the feature's exact location on the profile.

Reading a Trail Profile

Example using Profile 1A (reproduced above): The trail always begins at mile 0, at the left side of the profile. The trailhead is at Location Number [10], Big Oak Flat Road. The trail begins at an elevation of about 4,800 feet. At the one-mile mark, the elevation is about 5,300 feet. The trail dips at the 1.5 mile point, then rises and dips slightly at 1.8 miles, then again at 3.1 miles. At mile 4, there is a trail junction with the Rockslide Route, at Location Number [12]. The elevation at the junction is 6,000 feet. The trail continues to rise, to about 6,400 feet at mile 5, then levels off and continues irregularly past Location Number [8] to its end at Location [6], the Tamarack Creek Trailhead.

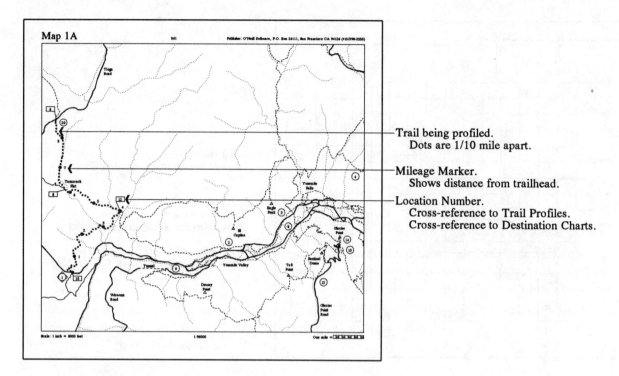

3.3 READING TRAIL MAPS

Trail Map Format

All Trail Maps are drawn to the same scale, 1 inch = 8000 feet, with true north to the top of the page. Maps show the profiled trail and its relationship to other trails, streams, lakes, peaks, passes, roads, and wilderness boundaries.

The trail being profiled is shown as a series of black dots. Distance from trailhead is shown in miles as a large dot with a mileage number alongside. Smaller dots are spaced one-tenth of a mile apart between mile markers. Dots represent "on-trail" distances, so they will be closer together on trails with switchbacks. If a trail has a lot of switchbacks, dots may even overlap. Distance between any two points along the trail can be determined by counting dots.

Significant features along the trail, such as trail junctions, lakes, and passes are shown by their Location Number inside a box. A line from the box points to the exact location on the trail from which distances (on Destination Charts and Trail Profiles) are measured.

Trail Maps show only a portion of the entire Yosemite Valley. You can get an idea of which portion is shown by looking at the bottom right corner of the trail's Profile Page. The small diagram labeled "Map Location" shows the main Yosemite Valley roads, and the Trail Map area in gray.

See the Map Legend on page 8 for an explanation of the symbols on Trail Maps. See the Key Map on page 9 for the location of all trailheads.

Reading Trail Map Distances

Example using Map 1A (reproduced above): Distance between points is read by counting dots. To determine distance from trailhead to Tamarack Flat Campground at Location Number [8]: There are 2 dots beyond Mileage Marker 6, so the distance is 6.2 miles. You can also determine distances, more precisely, by reading them from Destination Charts.

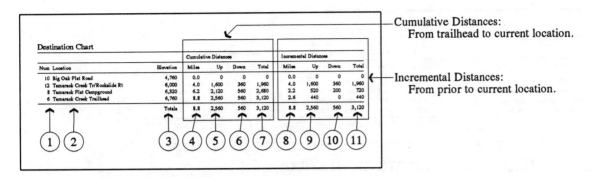

Cumulative Distances:
From trailhead to current location.

Incremental Distances:
From prior to current location.

3.4 READING DESTINATION CHARTS

Destination Chart Format

A Destination Chart lists significant features along a trail and tells how far each is from the trailhead and from each other. Only on-trail features are listed in Destination Charts. If a feature is not on or adjacent to a trail, it is not listed.

Distances shown are actual on-trail distances, horizontally and vertically. Distances are rounded to the nearest tenth of a mile. Elevations are rounded to the nearest 40 feet. Because distances are shown numerically, they are more precise than those interpolated from a Map or Profile.

Note that distances shown are what you actually hike, not just distances between points. For example, if distance up is shown as 500 feet, the actual location may be only 300 feet above you, but you have to hike up 500 feet (and down 200 feet) to get there.

Destination Charts show distances from two different perspectives. Cumulative Distances show distance and elevation gain or loss from the beginning of the trail to the current location. Incremental Distances show distance and elevation gain or loss from the prior location to the current location.

Column numbers are shown on the diagram above. Reading from left to right, Destination Chart columns show the following:

Column	Label	Shows
1	Num	Location Number of feature listed
2	Location	Location or feature name
3	Elevation	Elevation, in feet, of location or feature listed
4	Miles	Trail distance, in miles, from location to beginning of trail
5	Up	Elevation gain, in feet, from beginning of trail
6	Down	Elevation loss, in feet, from beginning of trail
7	Total	Sum of columns 5 and 6
8	Miles	Trail distance, in miles, from prior location to current location
9	Up	Elevation gain, in feet, from prior location to current location
10	Down	Elevation loss, in feet, from prior location to current location
11	Total	Sum of columns 9 and 10

Destination Chart

			Cumulative Distances				Incremental Distances			
Num	Location	Elevation	Miles	Up	Down	Total	Miles	Up	Down	Total
10	Big Oak Flat Road	4,760	0.0	0	0	0	0.0	0	0	0
12	Tamarack Creek Tr/Rockslide Rt	6,000	4.0	1,600	360	1,960	4.0	1,600	360	1,960
8	Tamarack Flat Campground	6,320	6.2	2,120	560	2,680	2.2	520	200	720
6	Tamarack Creek Trailhead	6,760	8.8	2,560	560	3,120	2.6	440	0	440
	Totals		8.8	2,560	560	3,120	8.8	2,560	560	3,120

3.4 READING DESTINATION CHARTS (CONTINUED)

Reading a Destination Chart

Example using Destination Chart 1A (reproduced above):

Line 1 shows the trailhead at Location Number [10], Big Oak Flat Road, at elevation 4,760 feet. All remaining columns are 0 because this is the beginning of the trail.

Line 2 shows that location [12], the junction of the Tamarack Creek Trail and the Rockslide Route, is at elevation 6,000 feet. You have to hike 4 miles, up 1,600 feet and down 360 feet from the trailhead to get here. Total loss and gain is 1,960 feet. The incremental distances are the same.

Line 3 shows that location [8], Tamarack Flat Campground, is at elevation 6,320 feet. To get here from the trailhead, you have to hike a total of 6.2 miles, going up 2,120 feet and down 560 feet. Total loss and gain is 2,680 feet. From the last trail junction, you will hike 2.2 miles, going up 520 feet, and down 200 feet.

Don't confuse net gain, which you might find in charts from other sources, with the elevation gains and losses shown in Destination Charts. Net gain is simply the difference between the start and end elevation. It ignores the ups and downs in between.

For example, the net elevation gain of Trail 1A is 2,000 feet (6,760 - 4,760). The actual elevation gain, from the Destination Chart, is 2,560 feet. The actual elevation gain includes the additional 560 vertical feet that must be hiked, up and down.

Using a Destination Chart While Hiking

The advantage of using a Destination Chart while hiking is that it gives you a quick summary of how far you've come and how far you must go.

Example using Destination Chart 1A (reproduced above): Let's say you are at location [8], at the Tamarack Flat Campground. You can tell immediately that you've climbed 2,120 feet in 6.2 miles, that you are at elevation 6,320, and that you have only 2.6 miles and 440 feet of gain to get to the Tamarack Creek Trailhead at Tioga Road.

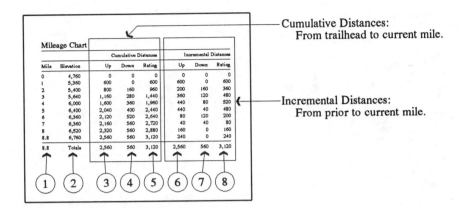

Cumulative Distances:
From trailhead to current mile.

Incremental Distances:
From prior to current mile.

3.5 READING MILEAGE CHARTS

Mileage Chart Format

A Mileage Chart shows elevation change on a per mile-basis. Because values are shown on a per-mile basis, they can be compared, directly, with other Mileage Chart values. In effect, a Mileage Chart provides a rating system for each mile along the trail. To emphasize that fact, headings in Mileage Charts are labeled Up, Down, and Rating instead of Up, Down and Total.

You can make logical comparisons using values in a Mileage Chart. For example, a trail that goes up 1000 feet in a mile is twice as steep as a trail that goes up only 500 feet.

Mileage Charts show distances from two different perspectives. Cumulative Distances show elevation gain and loss from the beginning of the trail to the current mile. Incremental Distances show elevation gain and loss from the prior mile to the current mile.

Column numbers are shown on the diagram above. Reading from left to right, Mileage Chart columns show the following:

Column	Label	Shows
1	Mile	Current mile
2	Elevation	Elevation, in feet, at current mile
3	Up	Elevation gain, in feet, from beginning of trail
4	Down	Elevation loss, in feet, from beginning of trail
5	Rating	Sum of columns 3 and 4
6	Up	Elevation gain, in feet, between prior and current mile
7	Down	Elevation loss, in feet, between prior and current mile
8	Rating	Sum of columns 6 and 7

Mileage Chart

Mile	Elevation	Cumulative Distances			Incremental Distances		
		Up	Down	Rating	Up	Down	Rating
0	4,760	0	0	0	0	0	0
1	5,360	600	0	600	600	0	600
2	5,400	800	160	960	200	160	360
3	5,640	1,160	280	1,440	360	120	480
4	6,000	1,600	360	1,960	440	80	520
5	6,400	2,040	400	2,440	440	40	480
6	6,360	2,120	520	2,640	80	120	200
7	6,360	2,160	560	2,720	40	40	80
8	6,520	2,320	560	2,880	160	0	160
8.8	6,760	2,560	560	3,120	240	0	240
8.8	Totals	2,560	560	3,120	2,560	560	3,120

Read the Mileage Chart a line at a time.
At mile 1, you've gone up 600 feet.

3.5 READING MILEAGE CHARTS (CONTINUED)

Reading a Mileage Chart

Example using Mileage Chart 1A (reproduced above):

Mile 0: This is the beginning of the trail. The elevation is 4,760 feet. You haven't gone anywhere on the trail yet, so the figures in the remaining columns are all 0.

Mile 1: The elevation is now 5,360 feet. In one mile, you've hiked up 600 feet. The incremental and cumulative distances are the same because this is the first mile. This mile had a rating of 600 feet.

Mile 2: The elevation here is 5,400 feet. In two miles, you've hiked up 800 feet and down 160. Between the last mile and this one, you've hiked up 200 feet (you hiked the first 600 feet during the first mile) and down 160. The rating for this mile is 360. This mile is about half as steep as mile 1.

Mile 3: The elevation here is 5,640 feet. In three miles, you've hiked up 1,160 feet and down 280 feet, for a total of 1,440 feet. Reading Incremental Distances, you can see that, between the last mile and this one, you've hiked up 360 and down 120 feet, for a total of 480 feet. The rating for this mile is 480 feet; harder than mile 2, but easier than mile 1.

Adjusting Mileage Ratings

Mileage Ratings shown in Mileage Charts are computed by adding elevation loss to elevation gain. That implies that hiking downhill is as hard as hiking uphill. You may feel that hiking downhill should make a rating easier, not harder. Or you may feel that elevation loss should just be ignored.

Mileage Ratings can be adjusted to your personal hiking style, as long as the adjustments are applied consistently. For example, if you feel that elevation losses should be ignored, just make the Up values your Mileage Rating. If you feel that going up is twice as hard as going down, you can multiply the Up value by two before adding it to the Down value. Any type of adjustment can be made, as long as it is applied consistently.

Mileage Chart

Mile	Elevation	Cumulative Distances			Incremental Distances		
		Up	Down	Rating	Up	Down	Rating
0	4,000	0	0	0	0	0	0
1	4,880	880	0	880	880	0	880
2	5,080	1,280	200	1,480	400	200	600
3	6,480	2,680	200	2,880	1,400	0	1,400
4	6,960	3,240	280	3,520	560	80	640
5	7,280	3,640	360	4,000	400	80	480
6	7,000	3,720	720	4,440	80	360	440
7	7,280	4,120	840	4,960	400	120	520
7.9	7,542	4,542	1,000	5,542	422	160	582
7.9	Totals	4,542	1,000	5,542	4,542	1,000	5,542

3D   Yosemite Falls Trailhead to North Dome

Mileage Chart

Mile	Elevation	Cumulative Distances			Incremental Distances		
		Up	Down	Rating	Up	Down	Rating
0	4,000	0	0	0	0	0	0
1	4,560	560	0	560	560	0	560
2	5,280	1,280	0	1,280	720	0	720
3	6,400	2,400	0	2,400	1,120	0	1,120
4	7,040	3,040	0	3,040	640	0	640
4.8	7,214	3,214	0	3,214	174	0	174
4.8	Totals	3,214	0	3,214	3,214	0	3,214

8A   Four Mile Trailhead to Glacier Point

3.6 RATING AND COMPARING TRAIL MILES

A Mileage Chart lets you rate and compare each mile along a trail. You can use Mileage Charts to compare individual miles or parts of different trails.

Comparing Individual Trail Miles

For this example, we'll see if the hardest mile from the Valley to North Dome is more difficult than the hardest mile from the Valley to Glacier Point. Assume we're taking the Yosemite Falls Trailhead to North Dome and the Four Mile Trail to Glacier Point. We'll use the Mileage Charts for trails 3D and 8A.

Since we are comparing individual miles, we use the Incremental Ratings, not the Cumulative Ratings. From Mileage Chart 3D, the hardest mile to North Dome is mile 3 with a rating of 1,400 feet. Mileage Chart 8A, to Glacier Point, also shows mile 3 as the most difficult, with a rating of 1,120. So, the hardest mile to North Dome is slightly more difficult than the hardest mile to Glacier Point.

Comparing Trail Segments

In this example, we'll determine which is more difficult, the first four miles to North Dome or the first four miles to Glacier Point. Here, we will use Cumulative Ratings because we are comparing more than one mile.

Looking at Mileage Chart 3D, to North Dome, we see that the Cumulative Mileage Rating at mile 4 is 3,520 feet. Mileage Chart 8A, to Glacier Point, shows a Cumulative Mileage Rating at mile 4 of 3,040 feet. The first four miles to North Dome are a little more difficult.

Remember, using Mileage Charts, you must compare the same number of miles on each trail. You can't logically compare four miles of one trail with three of another. Note that you can also compare trails by comparing their Profiles.

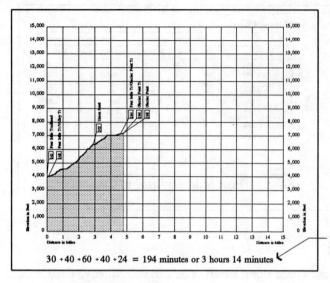

To estimate hiking time:
    Estimate time for each mile, then add for result.

$30 + 40 + 60 + 40 + 24 = 194$ minutes or 3 hours 14 minutes

3.7 ESTIMATING HIKING TIME

Here's a simple way to estimate the time to hike to any location. Hiking speeds can be broken down as follows:

Speed	Miles per Hour	Minutes per Mile	Minutes per Dot
Slow	1	60	6
Moderate	2	30	3
Fast	3	20	2
Very Fast	4	15	1.5

In other words, walking slowly, you can cover 1 mile in an hour, and it will take you 6 minutes to walk from one dot on the Trail Map to the next. Walking fast, you can cover the mile in 20 minutes, and it will take you only 2 minutes to walk from one dot to the next.

Using your trail's profile, put one of the above Minutes per Mile numbers beneath each mile on the graph, depending on how fast you expect to travel. Then just add the number of minutes for a total estimated time.

Example using Trail Profile 8A (reproduced above): Suppose you want to know how long it will take to hike from the Four Mile Trailhead to Glacier Point.

Look at the Profile's slope for the first mile (between mile 0 and 1). It's moderately steep. You can probably hike this mile at a moderate pace, so place 30 minutes between mile 0 and 1 at the bottom of the profile.

Look at the slope for the second mile (between mile 1 and 2). It is a little steeper than mile 1. Your pace will be slower, so place 40 minutes between the mile 1 and 2.

Mile three is quite steep. Your pace will be slow. Place 60 minutes between mile 2 and 3.

Mile four starts moderately steep and levels off. You can probably hike at a slow to moderate pace. Place 40 minutes between mile 3 and 4.

The final portion of the trail is not a full mile. It's about eight-tenths of a mile. If this distance was a full mile, you would place 30 minutes between mile 4 and 5. But the distance is only 0.8 miles, so multiply 0.8 by 30 to get 24 minutes. Place 24 minutes between mile 4 and 5.

Add the minutes: 30 + 40 + 60 + 40 + 24 = 194 minutes or 3 hours and 14 minutes.

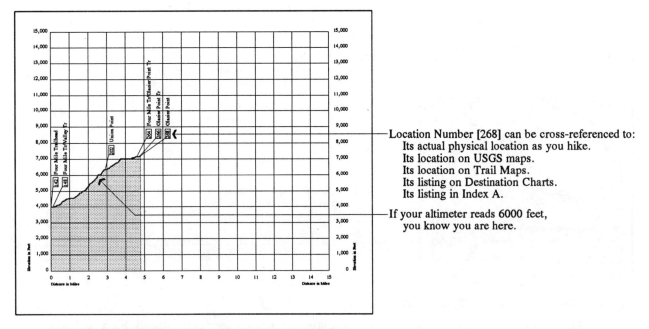

Location Number [268] can be cross-referenced to:
　Its actual physical location as you hike.
　Its location on USGS maps.
　Its location on Trail Maps.
　Its listing on Destination Charts.
　Its listing in Index A.

If your altimeter reads 6000 feet,
　you know you are here.

3.8 CROSS-REFERENCING TRAIL LOCATIONS

All *Trail Tools* views of a trail are based on the same points, and consequently, can be cross-referenced, not only to each other, but to the real-world as well.

For example, Location [268], Glacier Point, is shown at an elevation of 7,214 feet on Trail Profile 8A. The USGS 7.5 minute map of Half Dome shows it at the same elevation, which can be confirmed on trail by using an altimeter.

3.9 LOCATING CURRENT POSITION

Trail Tools can be used to locate your current position, track your progress, and get a feel for what will come next. You can locate your current position based on hiking speed or by using an altimeter.

Using Hiking Speed

You can use your hiking speed to calculate your approximate location, and the Trail Profile for a more exact fix.

Example using Profile 8A (reproduced above): Say you've been hiking for two hours on the Four Mile Trail and want to know where you are. Your hiking speed up steep hills is one mile per hour. You, therefore, must be two miles along the trail. The Profile shows your location at the two mile mark at about 5,200 feet elevation. Another mile and you will be at Union Point.

Using an Altimeter

You can use an altimeter along with a Trail Profile to locate your current position. Read the altimeter, then match the elevation reading with that on the profile.

Example using Profile 8A (reproduced above): Let's say your altimeter reads 6,000 feet. The Profile shows, at 6,000 foot elevation, that you've hiked about 2.5 miles from the Four Mile Trailhead. You have about 2 miles to go.

Using an altimeter to locate position works only where elevation change is fairly noticeable. If a trail is mostly level, all altimeter readings will be the same. If a trail goes through the same elevation several times, you need to estimate the distance you've already traveled to locate your current position.

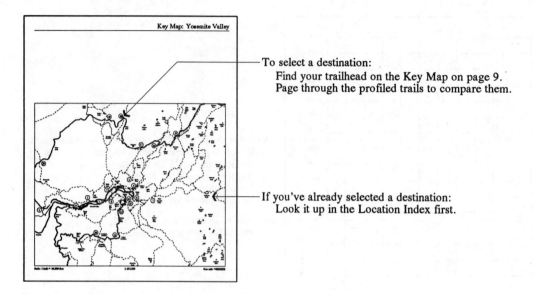

To select a destination:
   Find your trailhead on the Key Map on page 9.
   Page through the profiled trails to compare them.

If you've already selected a destination:
   Look it up in the Location Index first.

3.10 SELECTING A DESTINATION

Here's how to use *Trail Tools* to choose a destination from a specific trailhead. First find your trailhead on the Key Map on page 9. From there, turn to the appropriate trail number's Map Pages, beginning with the first, which ends with the letter A. You can tell at a glance where each trail from that point goes by looking the maps that follow. Then review and compare maps, profiles, and charts to make your selection. Some routes will have to be pieced together because they consist of more than one profiled trail. Joining trails is discussed in Section 3.12.

For example, select Trailhead 3 from the Key Map and look at map 3A, which begins at the Yosemite Falls Trailhead. Trail 3A goes to Tioga Road. Trails 3B and 3C also go to Tioga Road, at different locations. Look at the profiles to compare them. If you want to go to Yosemite Creek Campground instead of all the way to Tioga Road, just ignore the profile and map information beyond the campground. Flip pages beyond 3C for additional destinations.

3.11 BEST ROUTE TO A DESTINATION

In an area like Yosemite Valley, there are usually many routes to a destination. Choosing the best route depends on your criteria for selection, which can include just about anything you can think of. This book will help evaluate measurable criteria like distance and elevation gain.

The best way to select a route is to begin by looking up your destination in the Location Index, where features are listed in alphabetical order by name. If your destination is not listed, choose a nearby destination. The index lists all maps that profile a trail going to that destination. If you haven't selected a trailhead yet, look at each map, see where its trails go, compare profiles by flipping pages, and choose a route. If you already know where you want to start, limit your review to the trails from that trailhead.

For example, say you want to go to North Dome. The Location Index tells you that trails 3D, 4A, 5D, and 17C go to North Dome. Use the Destination Charts to compare distances from the different trailheads to North Dome. 3D shows 7.9 miles, 5D shows 10 miles, and 17C shows 5.5 miles. 4A is the same as 5D in the opposite direction. You can get an idea of how the trails differ by flipping back and forth between pages to compare profiles. You may want to use bookmarks to identify the pages.

Some routes will have to be pieced together because they consist of more than one profiled trail. Joining trails is discussed in Section 3.12.

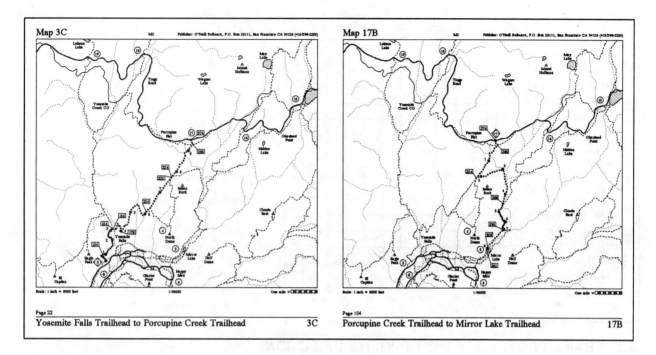

Yosemite Falls Trailhead to Porcupine Creek Trailhead   3C

Porcupine Creek Trailhead to Mirror Lake Trailhead   17B

3.12 JOINING TRAILS

To follow a long trail from beginning to end, or to follow a route that's not completely profiled, you have to join trails. The easiest way to join trails is to look up locations and common trail junctions in the Indexes.

For example, suppose you want to hike from the Yosemite Falls Trailhead to Mirror Lake via the Indian Ridge Trail. Look at Trail Map 3C, which goes most of the way. You want to take the Indian Ridge Trail beginning at Location [324]. You need to find a trail that goes from Location [324] to Mirror Lake, so look at Index A, the Location Index, for [324]. Nine different trail maps are listed, from trailheads 3, 4, 5, and 17. Since you will be heading toward trailhead 5, and from trailhead 3, you don't need to bother looking at those. Trails 4A and 17B each contain a segment from [324] to Mirror Lake, exactly what you want.

Here's your solution: Use Trail 3C from the trailhead to [324] and use 4A or 17B from [324] to Mirror Lake.

When you read a trail that is divided between two maps, profiles, or charts, consider only the portion of trail before the common trail junction on the starting end, and after the junction on the ending end. Ignore everything else.

Using the above route as an example: On Trail Map 3C, look only at the portion of trail from the trailhead to location [324]. Ignore the rest. On Trail Map 17B, look only at the portion of trail from Location [324] to the end of the trail.

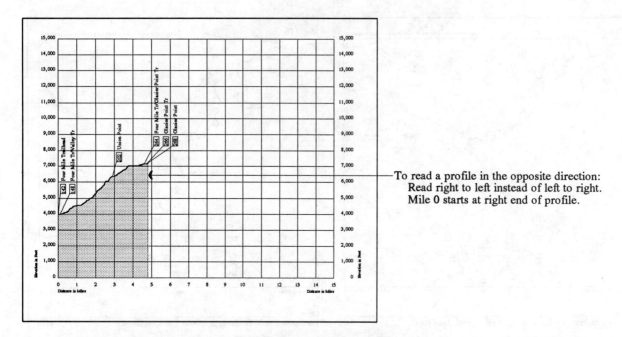

To read a profile in the opposite direction:
  Read right to left instead of left to right.
  Mile 0 starts at right end of profile.

3.13 TRAILS PROFILED IN THE OPPOSITE DIRECTION

Although most trails are profiled in both directions, there will be times when a trail is profiled in one direction and you are heading in the opposite direction.

If you are reading a Trail Map of a trail profiled in the opposite direction, the small dots, indicating tenths of a mile spacings are valid, but the Mileage Marker numbers are not. You can ignore them or count dots and place a new set of large dots at every tenth dot, starting at your Trailhead. Location Numbers, of course, are still valid and constant throughout.

To read a profile from the opposite direction, just assume you are going from right to left instead of left to right. The profile itself, and none of the Location Numbers change, but distances along the bottom must be revised. Zero must start on the right, not the left.

Destination Charts for trails profiled from the opposite direction must be read from the bottom up instead of top down. Distances labeled as Up are now Down, and distances labeled Down are now Up. Elevations and Incremental Distances are still valid but Cumulative Distances are not. The same changes must be applied to Mileage Charts. In addition, although whole mile numbers are valid, fractional miles are not.

As an alternative to following trails in the opposite direction, you can order custom-designed *Trail Tools* pages, which will show any combination of trails, in the directions you choose. An order form is in the back of the book on page 143.

APPENDIX

ABOUT THE AUTHOR

I began plotting trail profiles, by hand, after I moved to California and began backpacking in the late sixties. As an architect, I was quite familiar with reading maps, extracting information, and portraying it graphically. Profiles let me, as a beginning backpacker, understand trails I had never been on, and gave me the confidence that comes with that knowledge. My accumulating collection of profiles provided memories of trips, and I also found them useful for comparing one trip with another. Later, when I began leading Sierra Club backpack trips, they became indispensable tools for selecting routes, planning trips, and preparing final trip reports.

Paralleling my growing interest in hiking, backpacking, and eventually, back-country skiing, was my interest in writing computer software. In the early eighties, I left architecture for a new career in computer software, and have been enjoying working with computers ever since.

Recently, I've managed to combine my favorite interests by developing software to produce trail profiles and other related information by computer. This book is the result. I hope it gives you what my earlier profiles gave me: knowledge, confidence, memories, and many enjoyable hours on trail.

ACKNOWLEDGMENTS

I've received advice, assistance, and support from many people. In particular, I'd like to acknowledge the following:

Yosemite National Park and Yosemite Association personnel for discussing maps, providing information, and answering my questions about the roads and trails in the park. I am especially grateful to the staff members at the Wilderness Office, the Roads and Trails Office, and the Research Library.

The staff at the U.S. Geological Survey, in Menlo Park, who provided me with invaluable information and patiently answered my questions about maps, map projections, map accuracy and other related topics.

Other map and book authors and publishers, who provided an abundance of advice. In particular, I am indebted to: Tom Harrison of Tom Harrison Cartography; Marcus Libkind of Bittersweet Publishing Company; Tom Winnett and Caroline Winnett of Wilderness Press.

My fellow Sierra Club trip leaders and hiking companions, for their comments and advice, especially Jim Watters, Bill Flower, Brent Pettey, Andy Westbom, and Marvin Johnson. Fellow members of the Pincrest Nordic and Lake Alpine Nordic Ski Patrols, for their enthusiastic support.

Especially, I want thank my closest companion, favorite backpack trip leader, trusted advisor, and wife, Roxann Hanning.

ORGANIZATIONS

Although wilderness areas appear everlasting, they are actually fragile environments that need protection. There are many ways you can help. Contact:

Wilderness Watch	406/542-2048
Wilderness Society	800/878-2301
Sierra Club	415/923-5653
Leave No Trace	800/332-4100
Desert Survivors	510/769-1706
Yosemite Association	209/379-2646

REFERENCES

Maps

The trails and profiles in this book were based on the following 7.5 minute USGS maps:

Map	Date
Yosemite Falls	1992
El Capitan	1990
Tenaya Lake	1992
Half Dome	1990
Merced Peak	1990
Tamarack Flat	1990

Additional information was obtained from the following maps:

Map	Date	Publisher
Yosemite High Country	1995	Tom Harrison Cartography
Yosemite National Park	1986	Wilderness Press

Books

Additional information was obtained from the following:

Yosemite National Park, Jeffrey P. Schaffer, 1983, Wilderness Press

Yosemite Official Map and Guide, National Park Service brochure, 1990

Above Yosemite, Robert Cameron, 1983, Robert W. Cameron and Company, Inc.

INDEX A: BY LOCATION NUMBER

This index includes names of trails, trail junctions, and features along a trail, listed in order by Location Number. Two pieces of information are provided for each Location Number: its location name and a list of trails that go to or by the indexed location. For an alphabetical listing of locations, see Index B.

INDEX B: BY LOCATION

This index includes names of trails, trail junctions, and features along a trail. Two pieces of information are provided for each indexed location: its Location Number, in brackets, and a list of trails that go to or by the indexed location.

Listings are in alphabetical order by location or trail name. Where appropriate, locations are listed under two or more names. *For example, Location [368] is listed under both John Muir Tr/Mist Tr and Mist Tr/John Muir Tr.* Trail names themselves don't have Location Numbers.

CUSTOM TRAIL TOOLS ORDER FORM

INSTRUCTIONS:

- ☐ Make a copy of the Key Map (or any other map in this book).
- ☐ Circle start location, end location, and overnight points.
- ☐ Mark your route. Show direction of travel with arrows.
- ☐ Mail this form with your marked-up maps to:

    O'Neill Software
    P.O. Box 26111
    San Francisco, CA 94126

- ☐ We'll call, fax, or email you a price quote. Normal charges are $3 per order. Routes greater than 10 miles may require additional pages at $1 per page.
- ☐ After you approve the price quote, we'll prepare the Custom pages and fax or mail them to you. Mailed pages will be printed on white paper similar to that used for making xerox copies, folded and mailed in a normal business envelope, unless you provide special handling instructions below.

Send Custom Trail Tools ☐ via mail ☐ via fax to:

Name: _____

Company Name: _____

Address: _____

City: _____ State: _____ Zip: _____

Phone: (_____)_____ Fax: _____ Email: _____

- ☐ Special Handling Instructions:

Price Quote: _____ Date: _____

    I understand that Custom Trail Tools are intended for personal non-commercial use only. I agree not to sell or distribute them commercially without O'Neill Software's prior written permission.

Signed: _____ Date: _____

Questions? Call 415/398-2255 or send email to oneillsw@hooked.net

MAILING LIST/BOOK ORDER FORM

Name: _____

Company Name: _____

Address: _____

City: _____ State: _____ Zip: _____

Phone: (_____)_____ Fax: _____ Email: _____

Date: _____

☐ Please add my name to your mailing list. Notify me of new *Trail Tools* books and special discount offers.

☐ Please let me know when *Trail Tools* for _____ are available.

☐ Please rush me a copy of *Trail Tools: Yosemite Valley* @ $12.95 per book $_____

☐ Please rush me a copy of *Trail Tools: Desolation Wilderness* @ $16.95 per book $_____

    For Book Orders:

        Sales Tax @ 7% for shipments to California $_____

        Shipping (*choose one of the rates below*)

            ☐ Book Rate @ $2.00 (may take 3 to 4 weeks): $_____

            ☐ First Class Rate @ $4.00: $_____

      ☐ Check enclosed for total amount: $_____

Mail this form (with your check if you ordered a book) to:

O'Neill Software
P.O. Box 26111
San Francisco, CA 94126

415/398-2255
Email: oneillsw@hooked.net